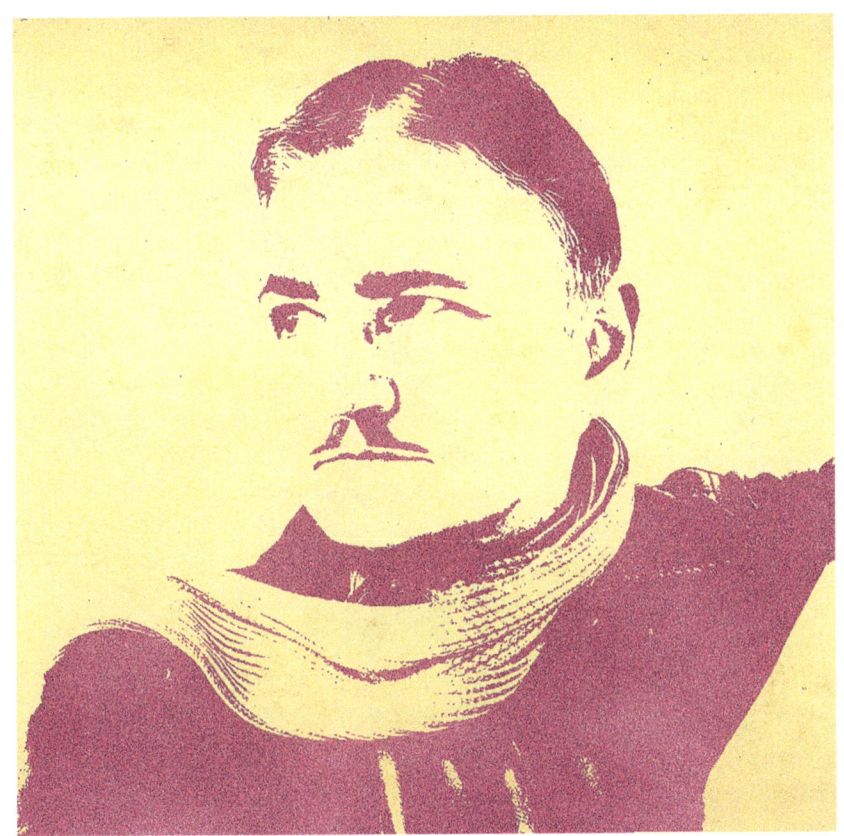

Stanley Studio
StanleyStudio.com
info@stanleystudio.com

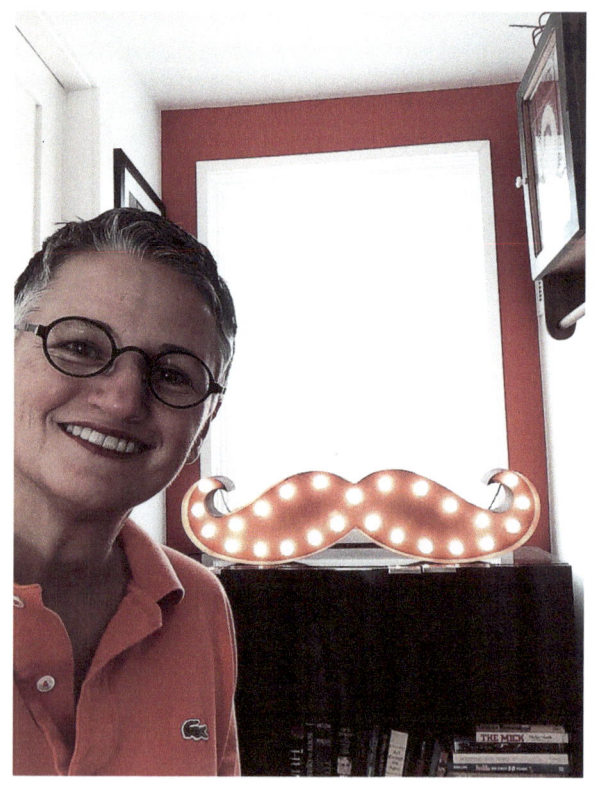

S. Van Lokey was born and raised in Dallas. She received a Bachelor of Fine Arts in painting and drawing from the University of North Texas in 1988.

While painting is her first love, Lokey has been very involved in photography for the past few years.

Lokey has always enjoyed playing characters, and this project seemed like a natural step.

info@stanleystudio.com

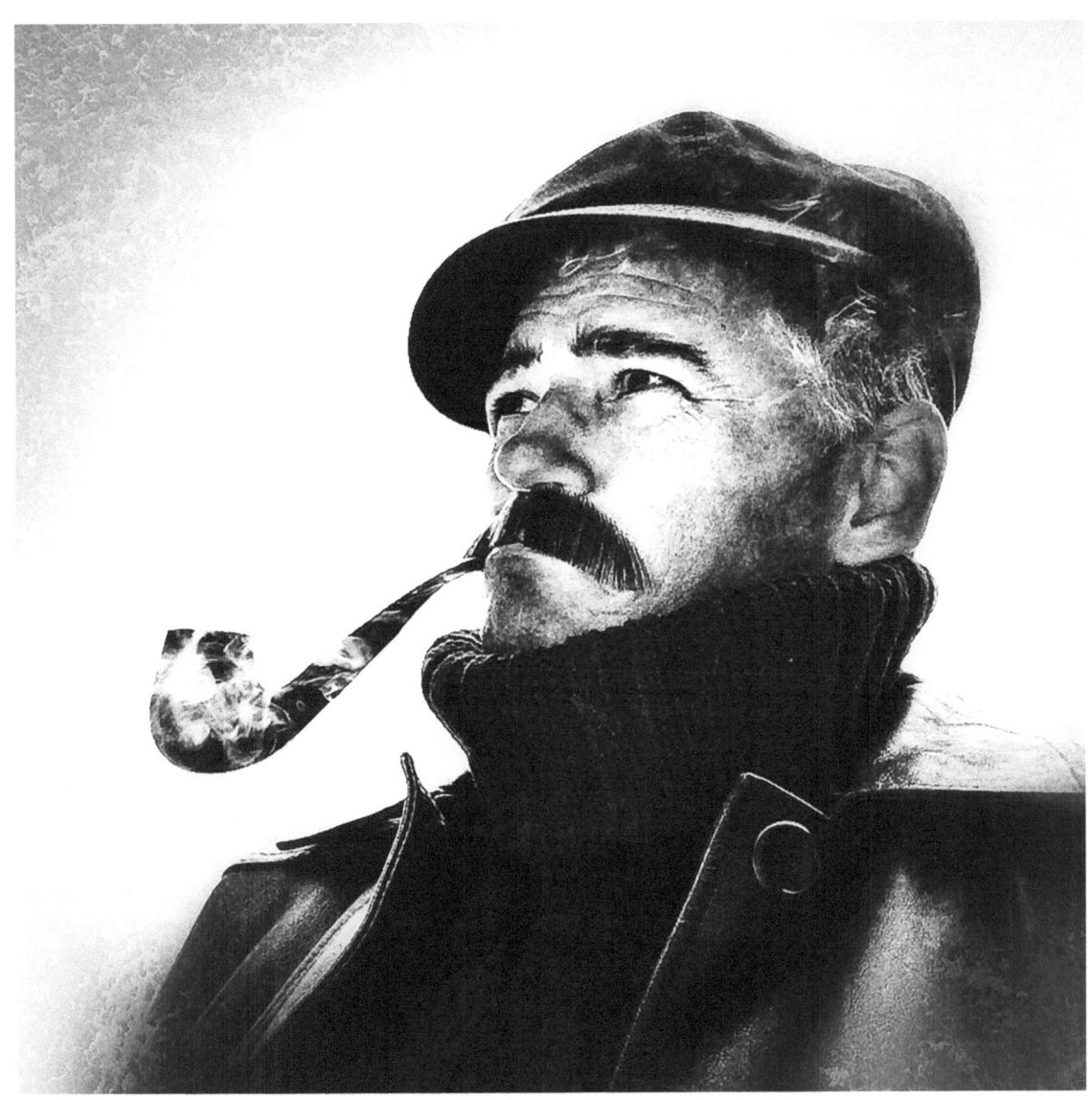

Ernest H. Van der Lokey, III

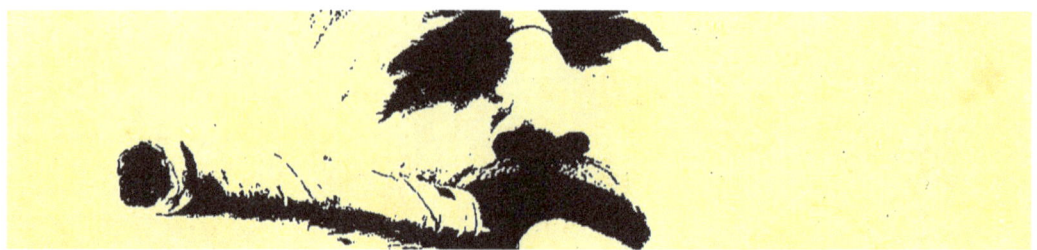

What started out as a wacky Movember moustache photo project quickly turned into a serious exercise in making me unrecognizable even to myself. My original plan was to take outrageous photos of me wearing different color moustaches while making silly faces, but that quickly got old. The project took on a life of its own when I started using props to "get into character".

I took all of the photos in this book on my iPhone 5s. I did not digitally alter my face; I used stick-on moustaches, eyebrow liner and face paint to create the characters. I then used a few iPhone apps to get the desired effect. For most of the photos, I reduced the color saturation, and I adjusted the contrast and lighting. I also combined some "vintage" filters to create the overall look.

I had a great time working on this project and I hope you enjoy the results.

For the month of November, AKA, Movember, men grow moustaches for charity to raise awareness and funds for men's health. You don't have to grow one to wear one.

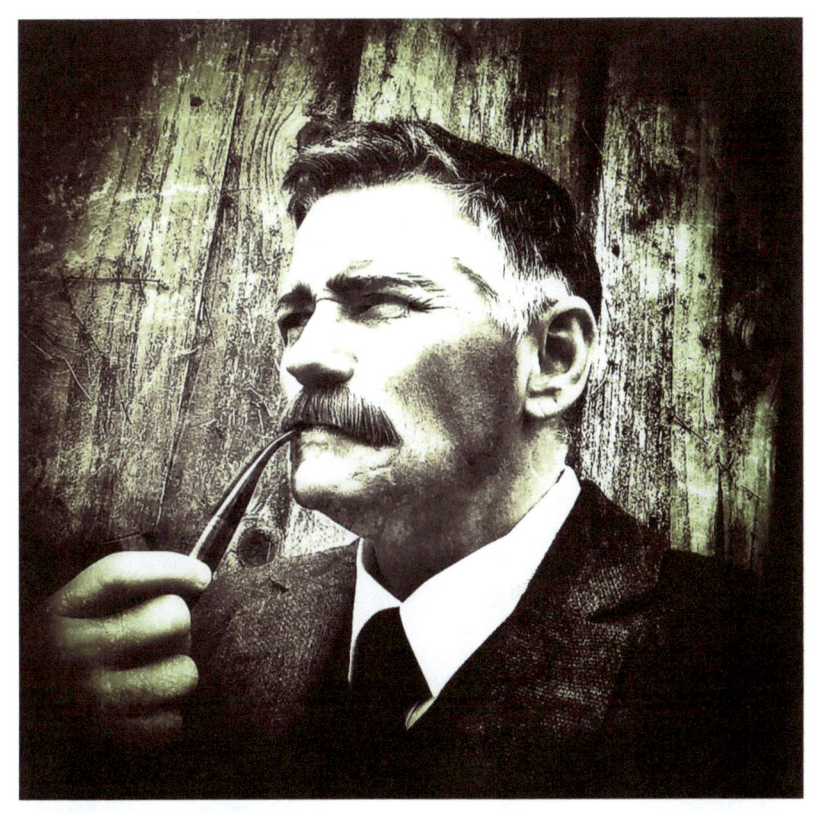

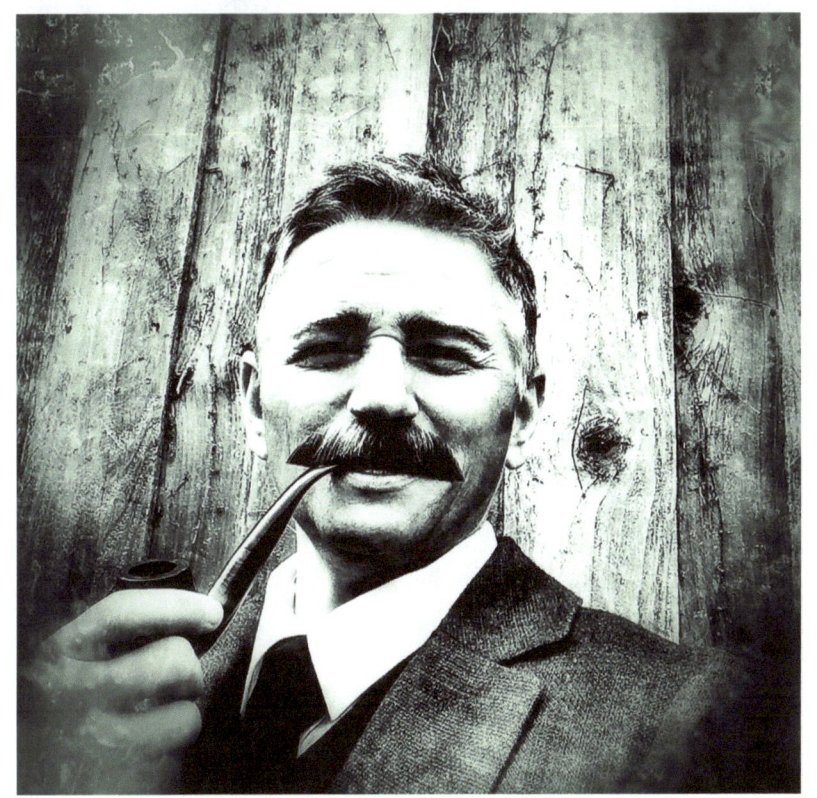

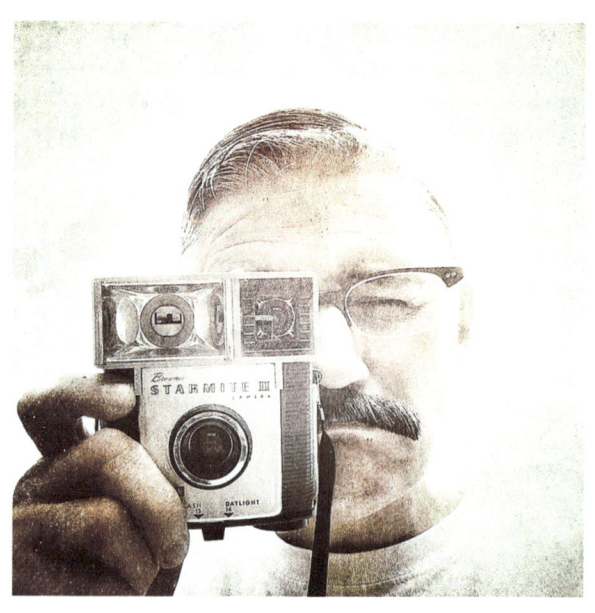 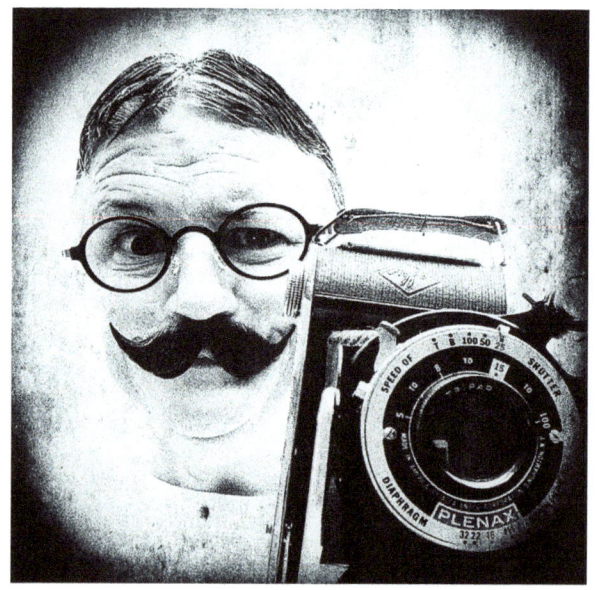

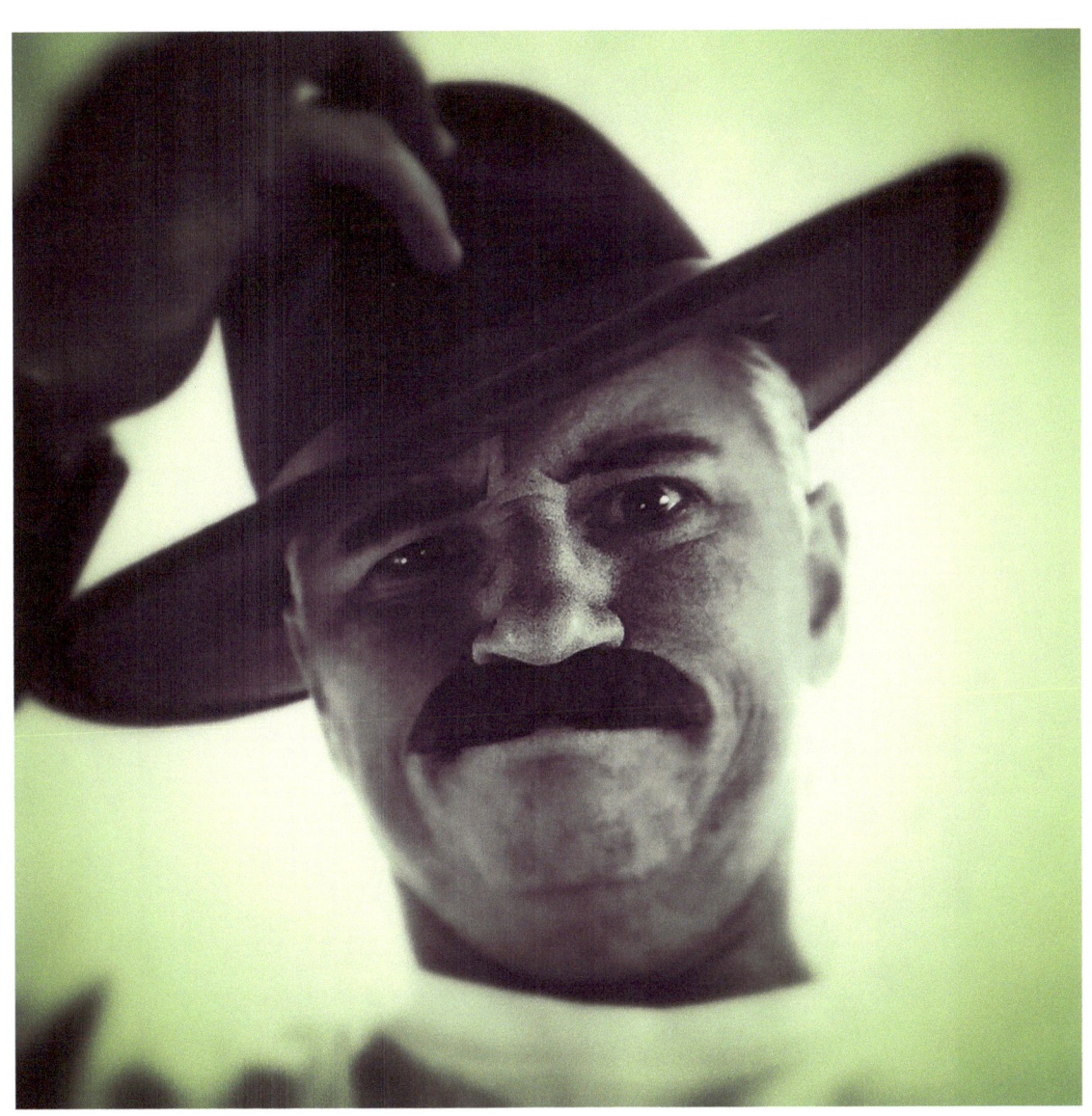

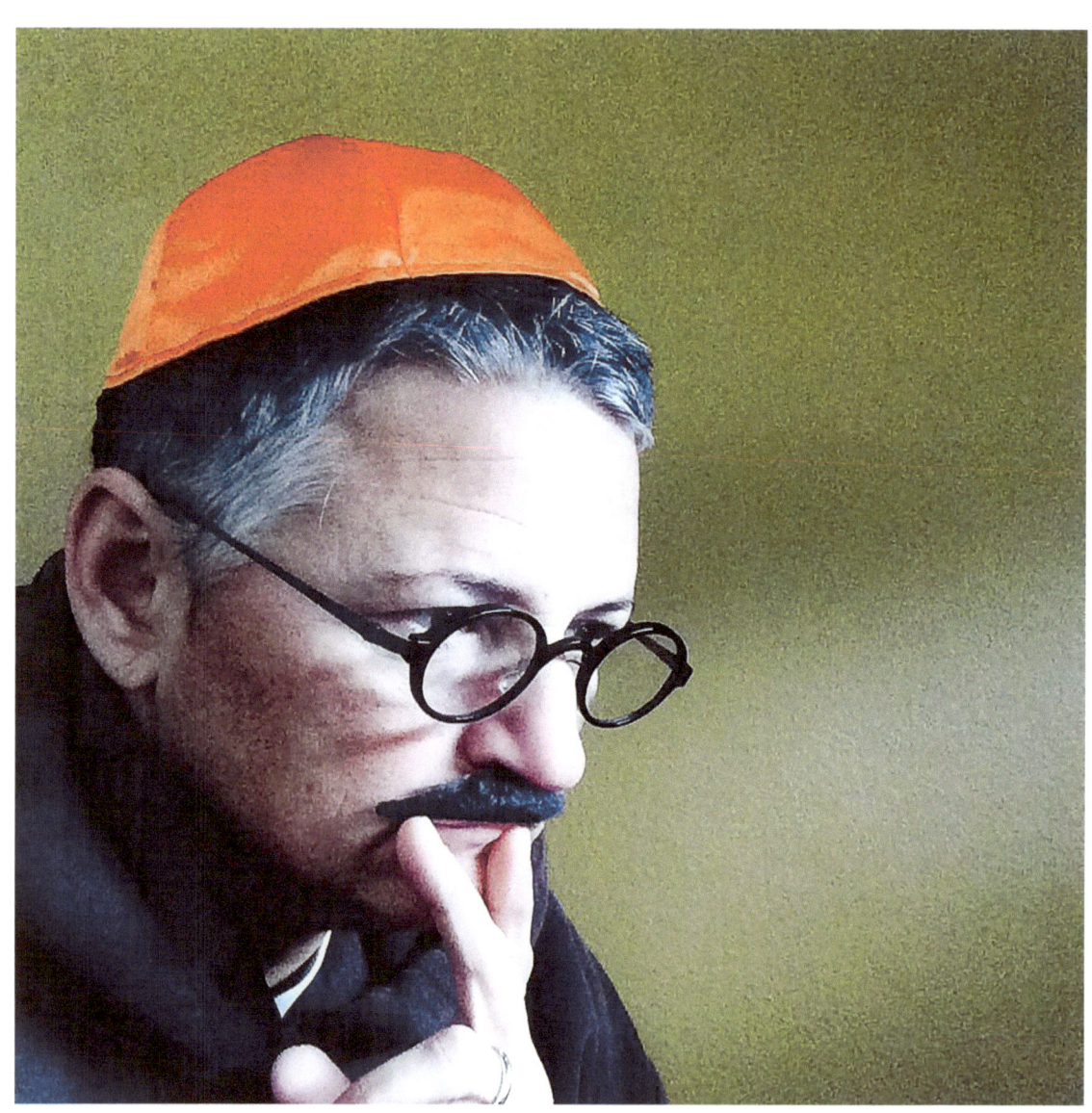

Pope Moustacho, III

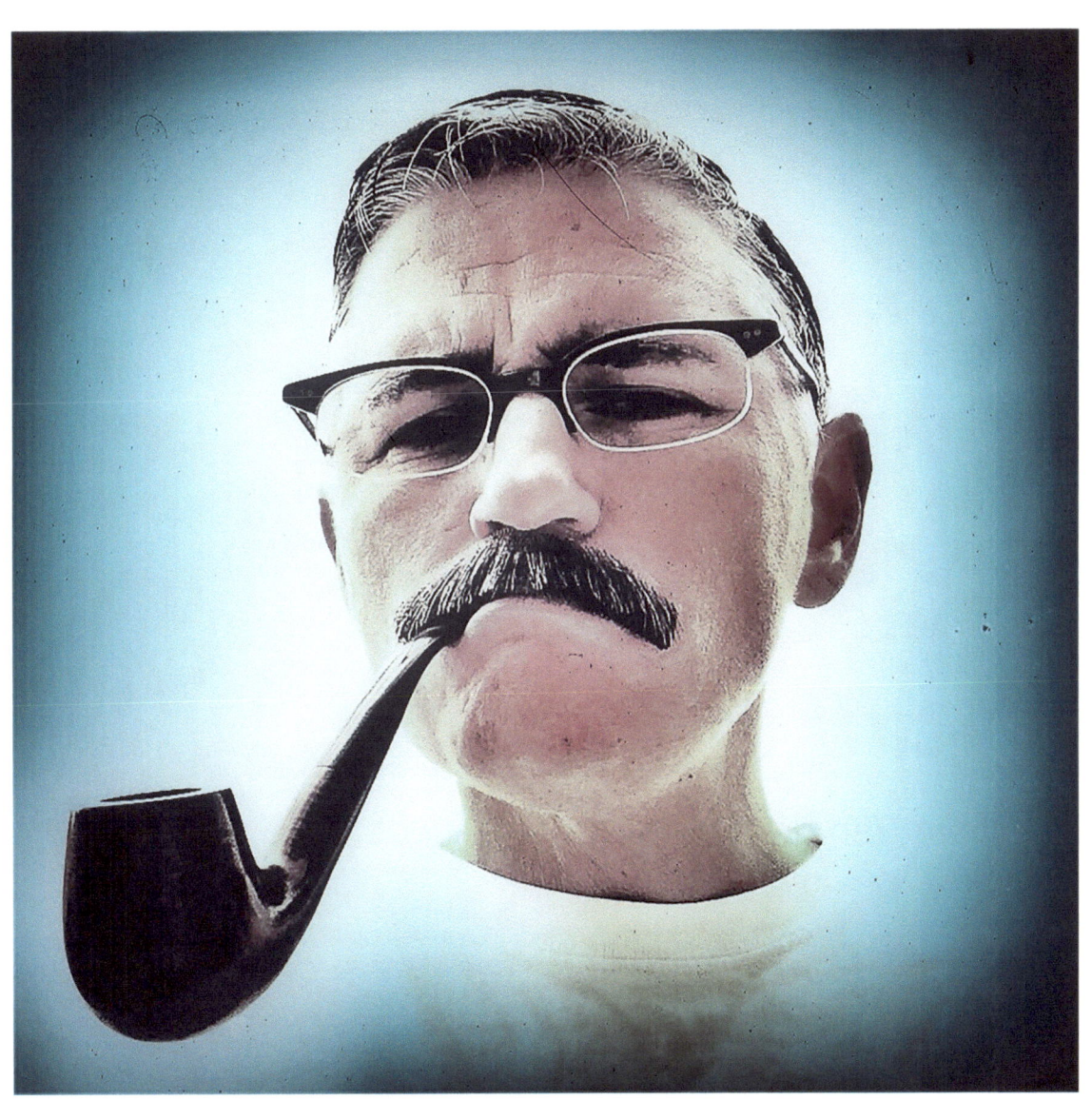

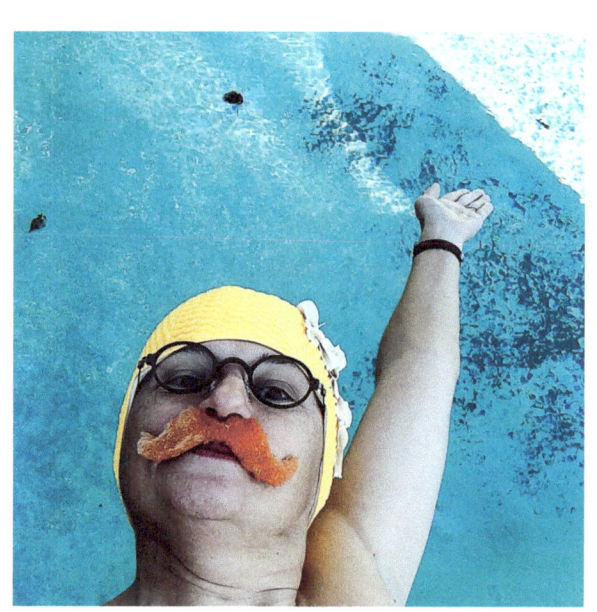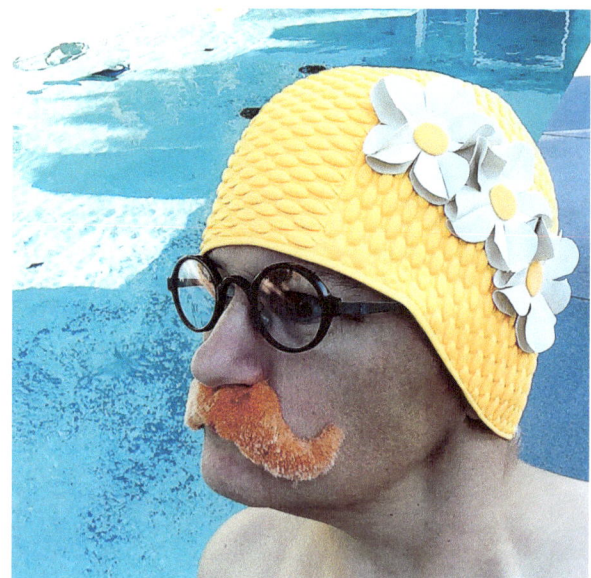

E. William Van der Lokey, III

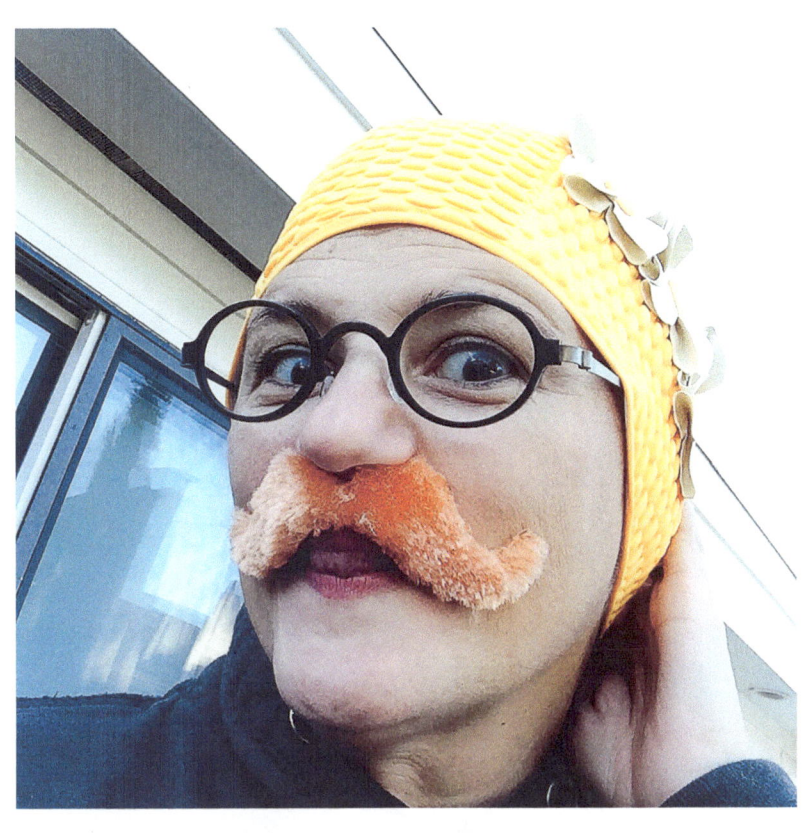

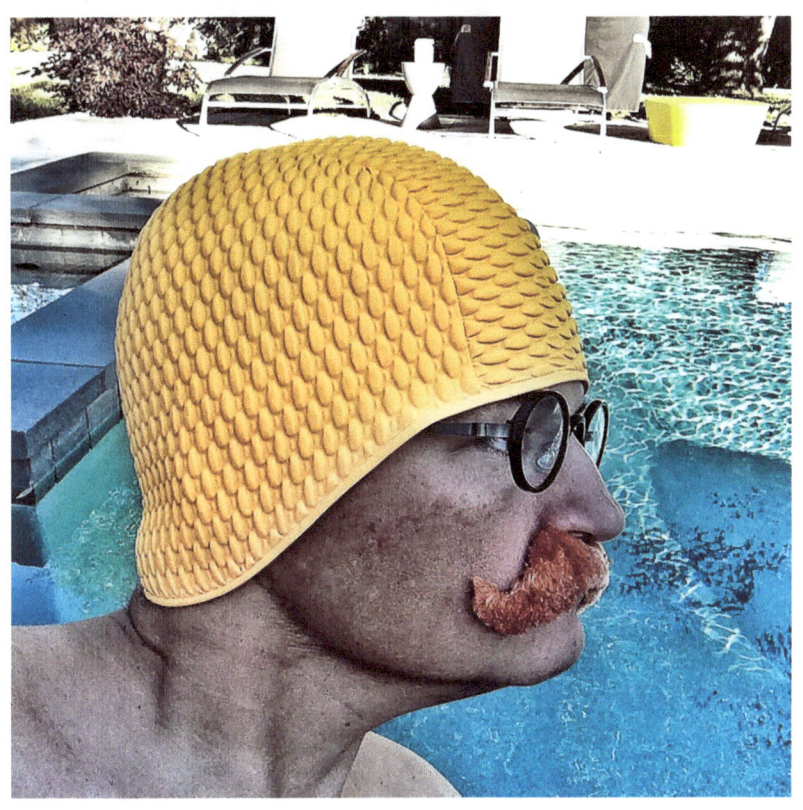

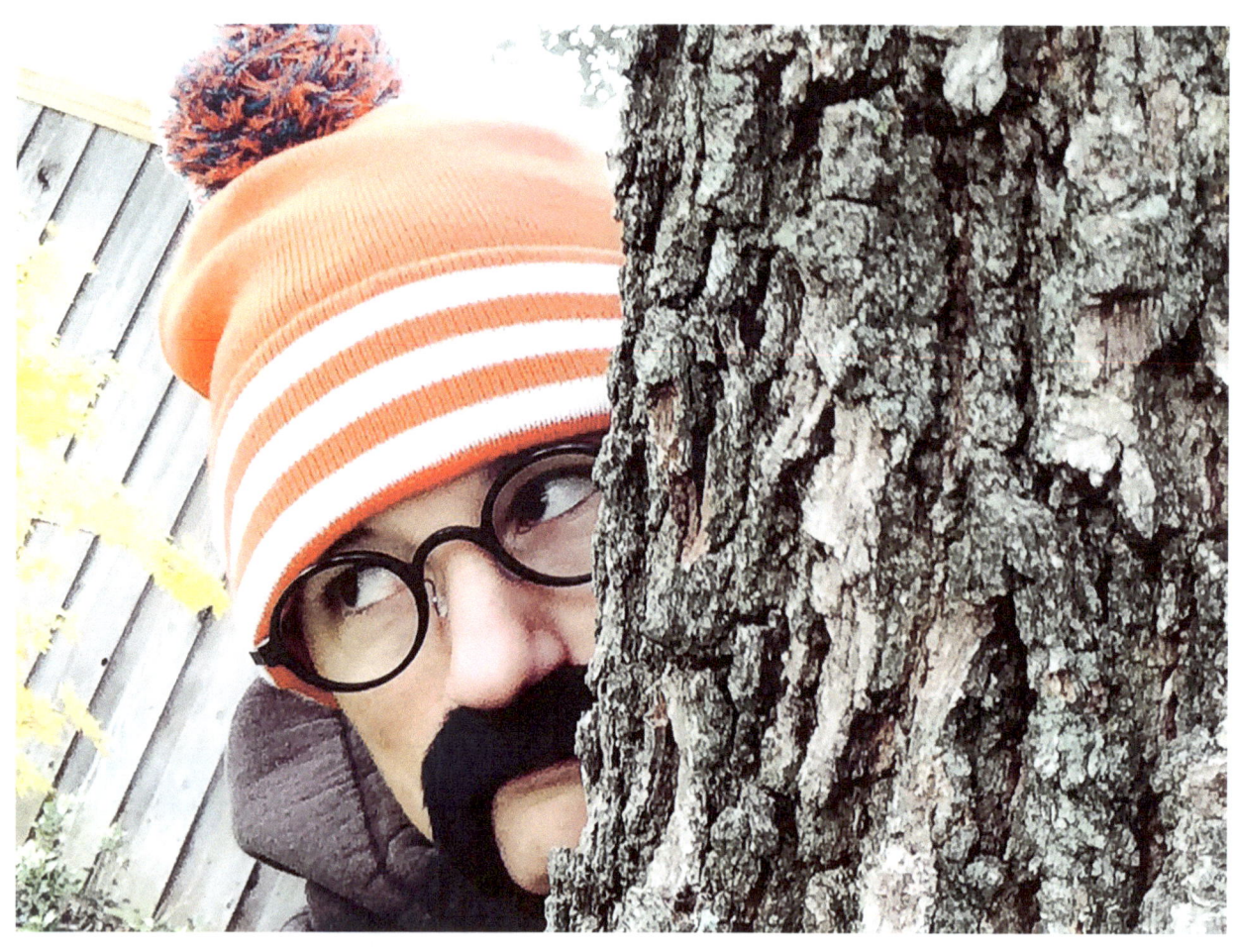

Waldo Van der Lokey, III

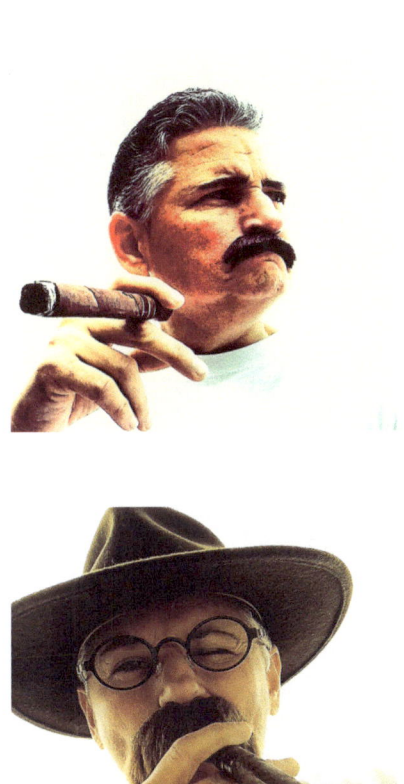

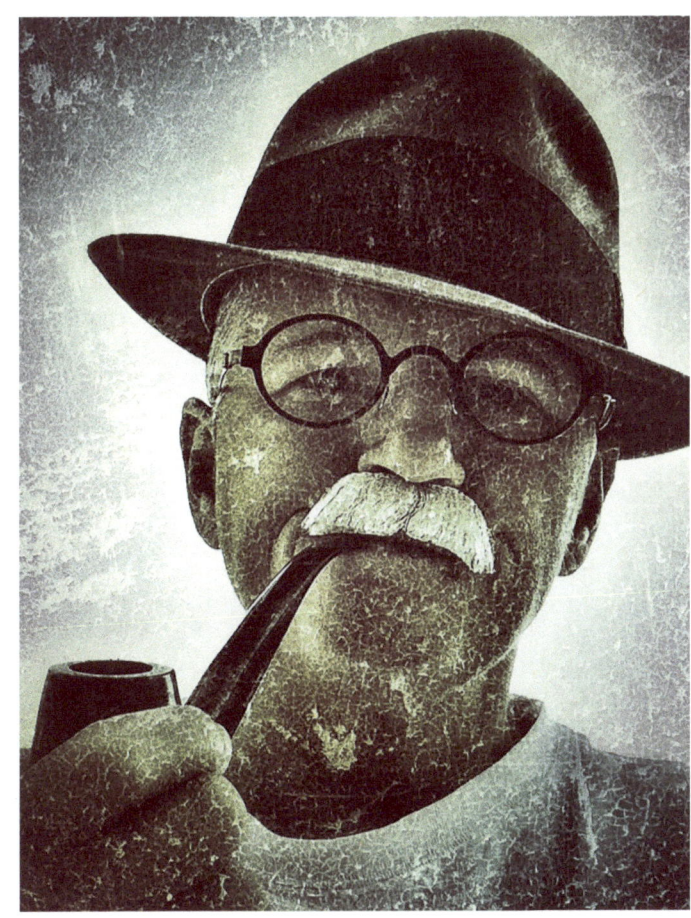

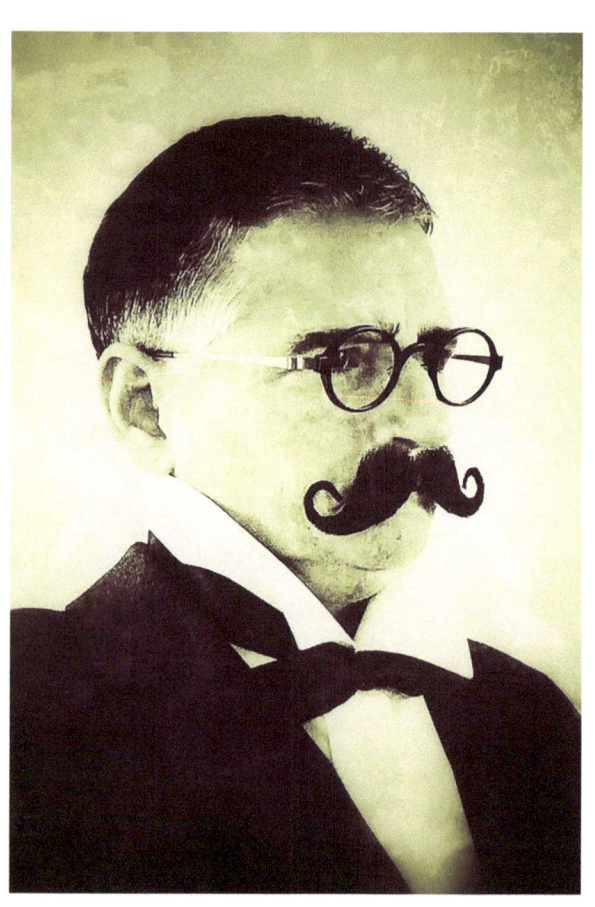 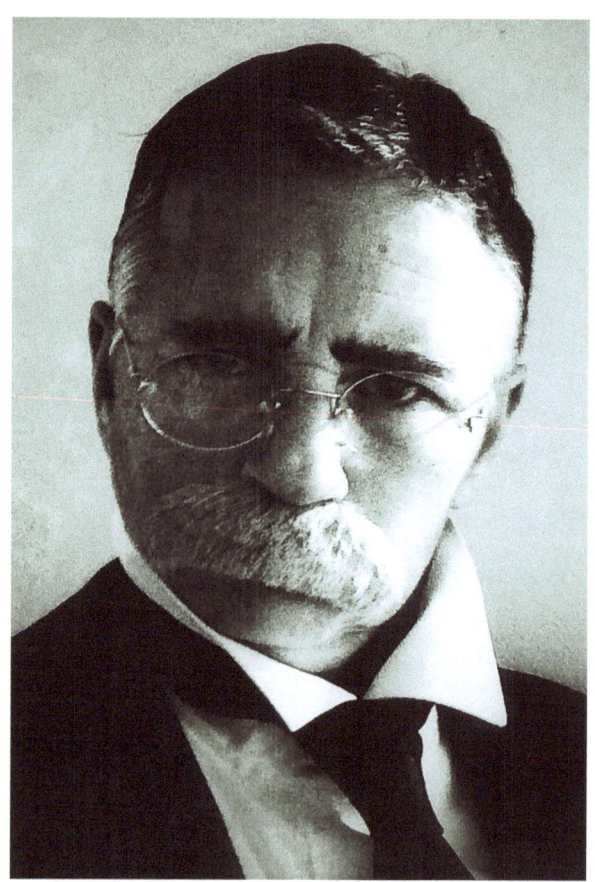

Clarence Van der Lokey, III   Theodore Van der Lokey, III

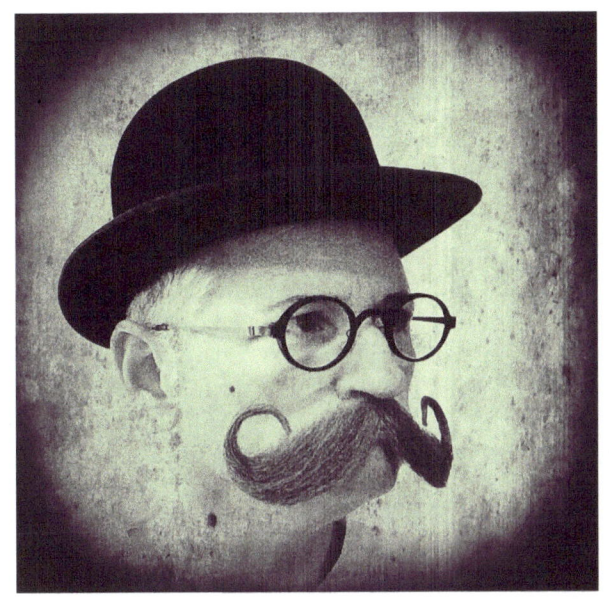
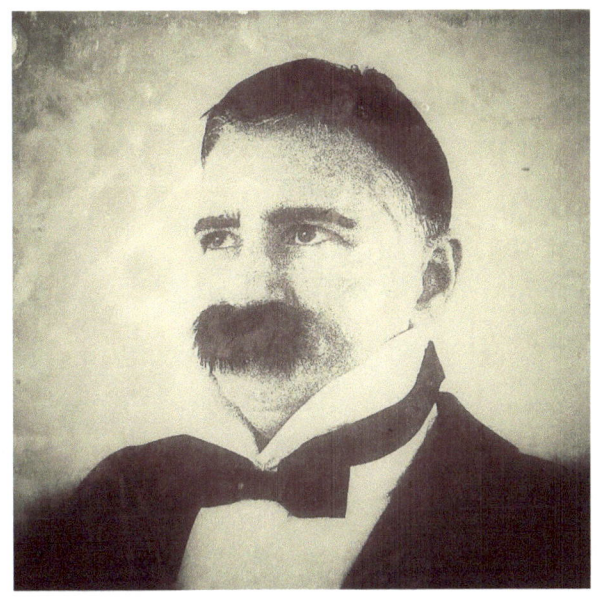
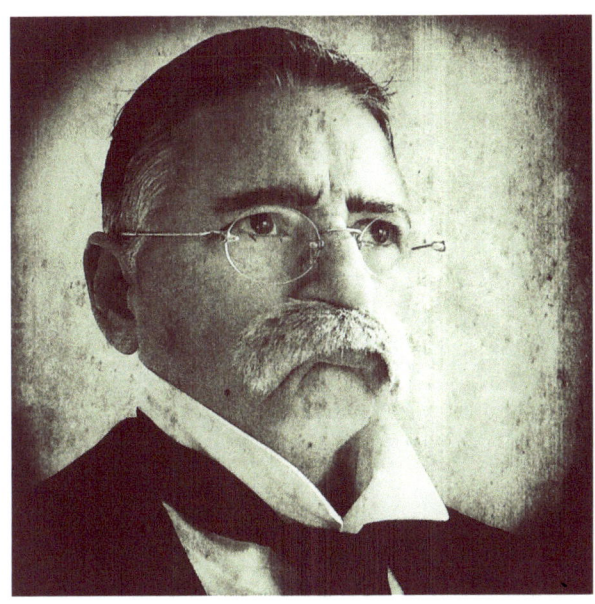
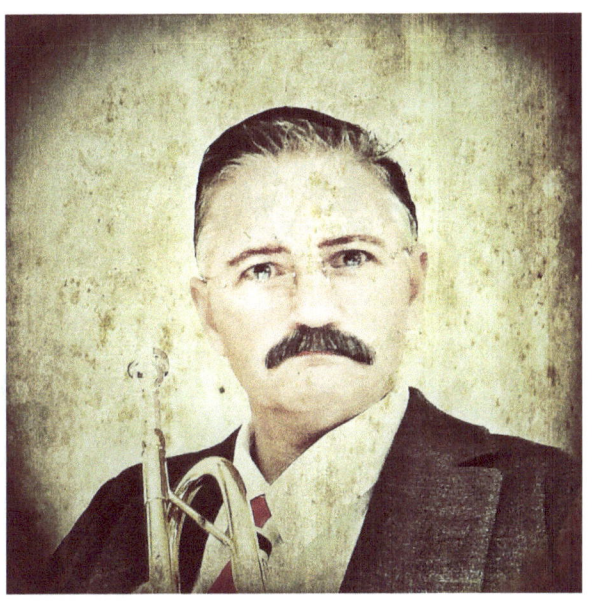

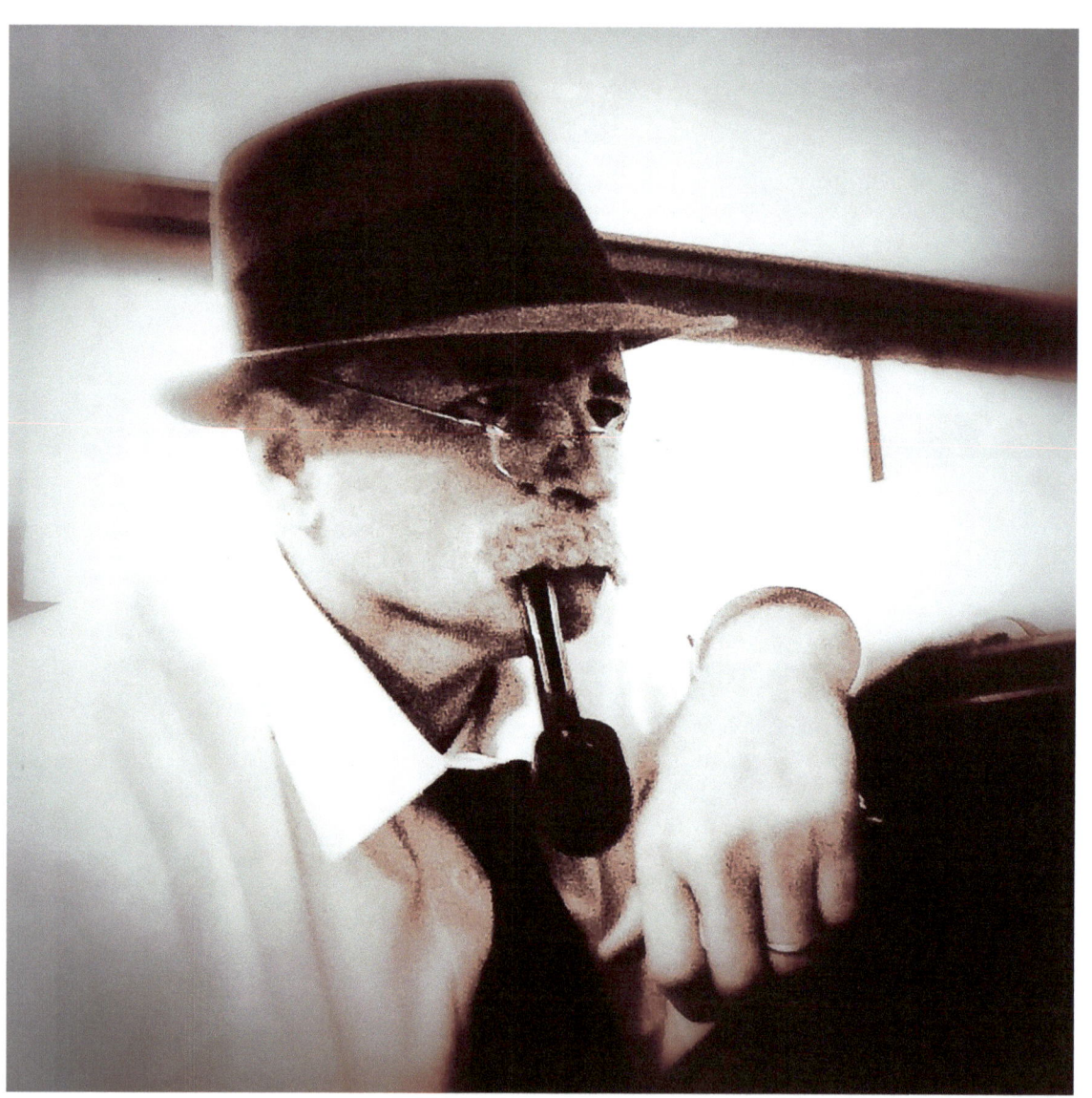

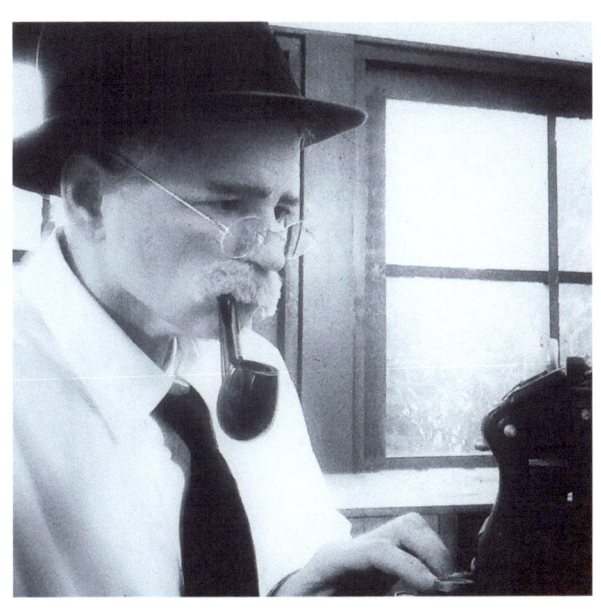
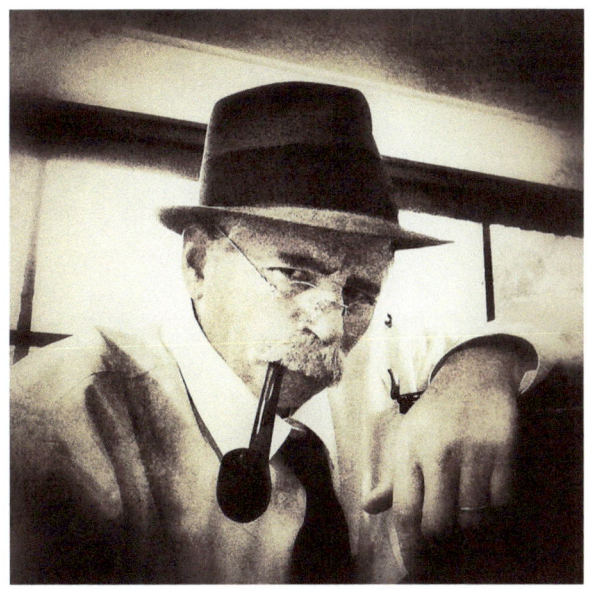

Frank Van der Lokey, III

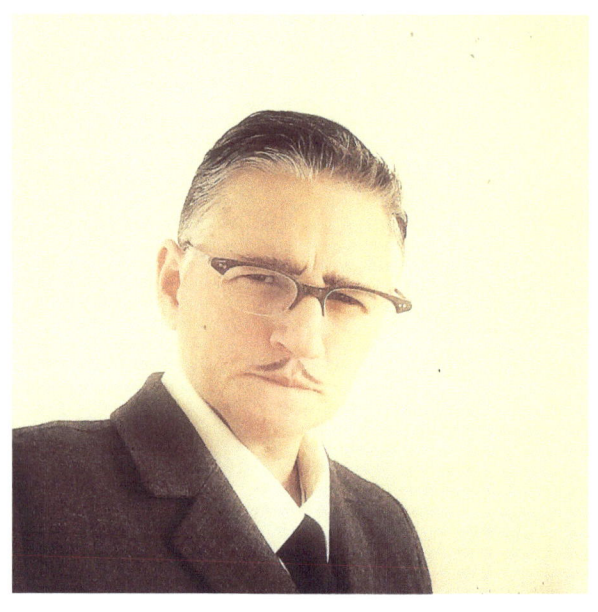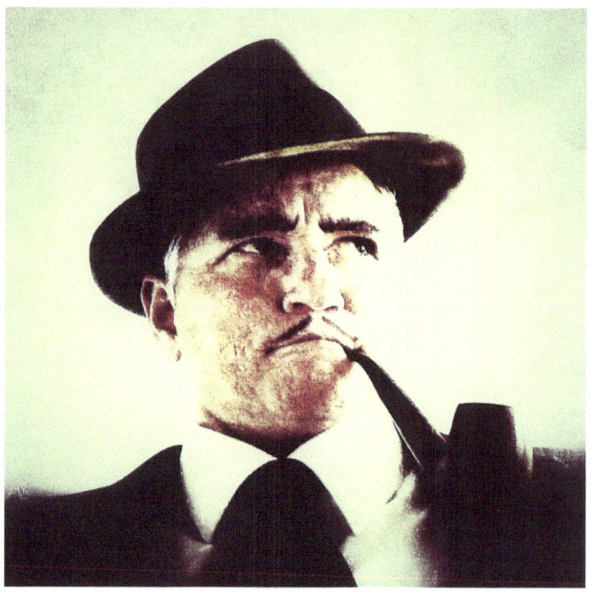
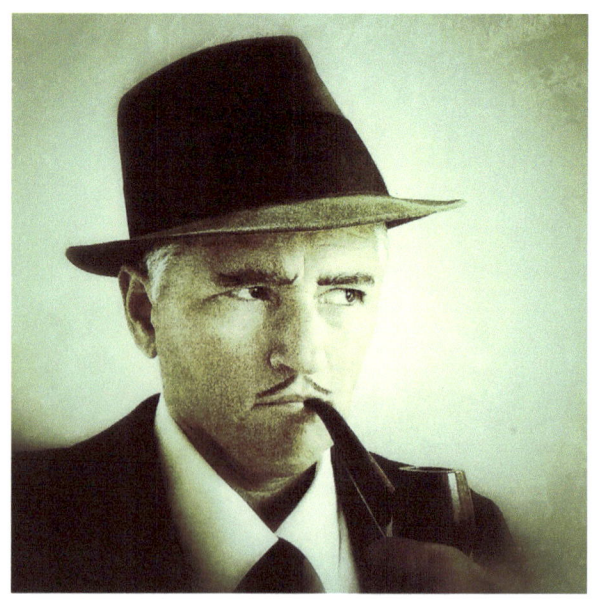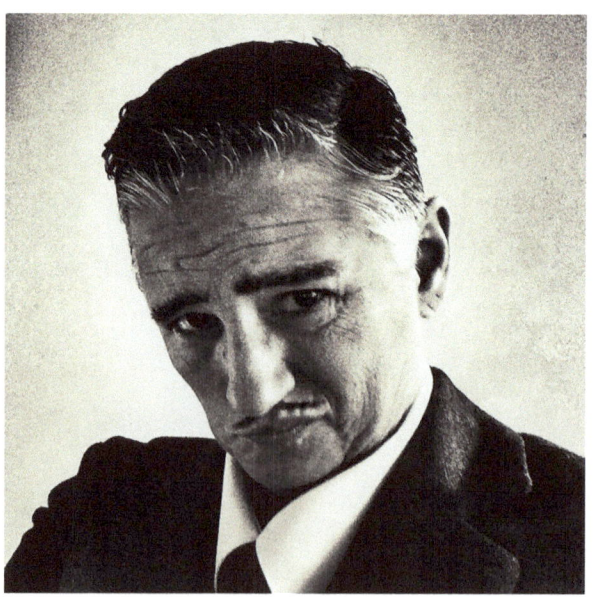

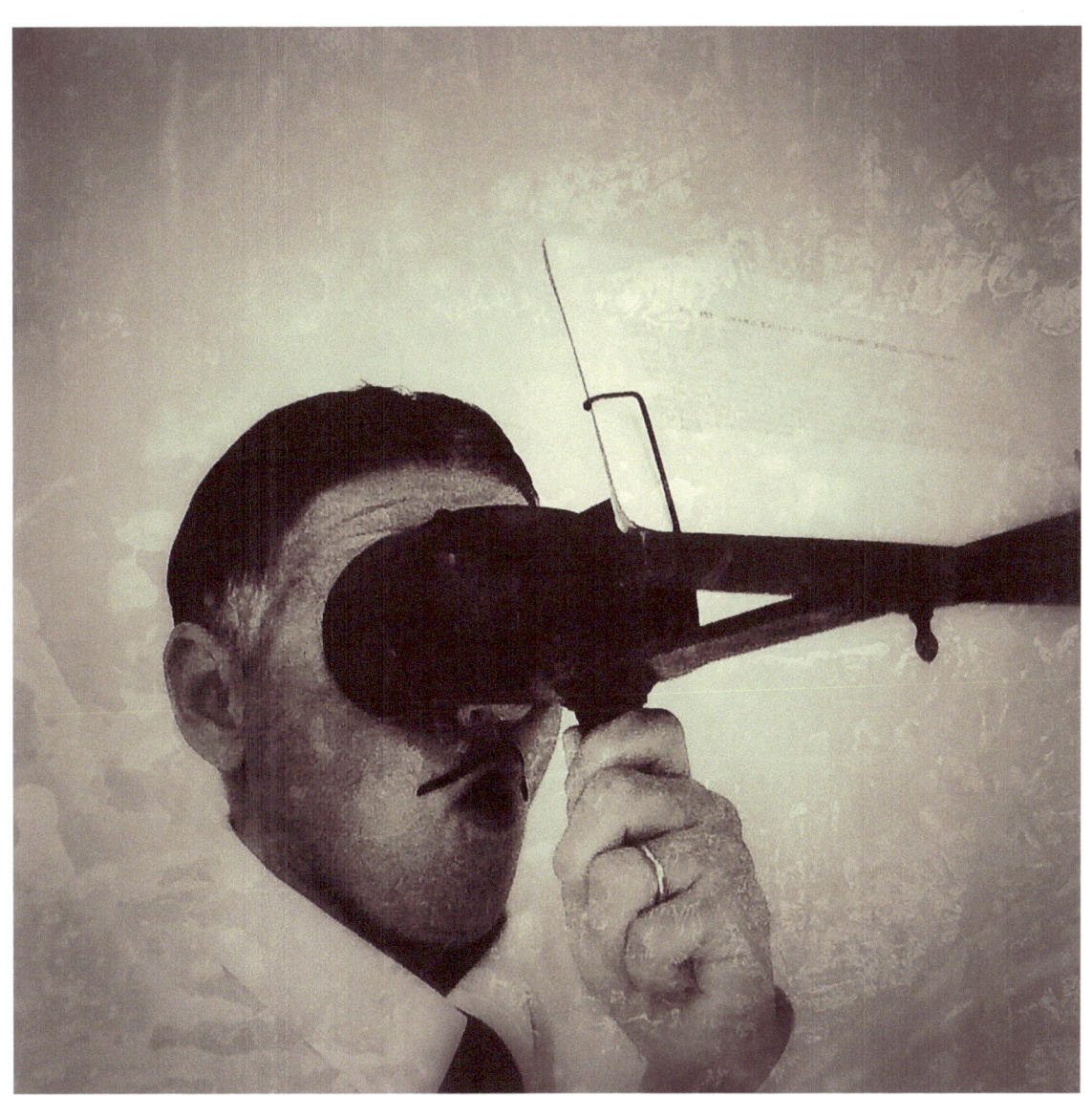

Cornelius Van der Lokey, III
Inventor of the pornoscope.

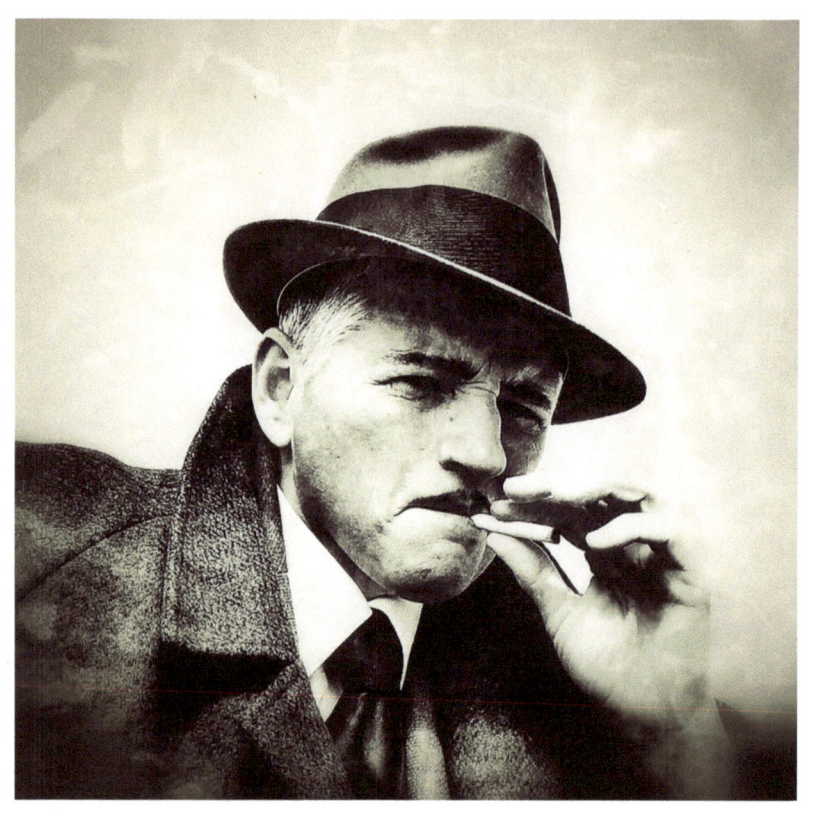

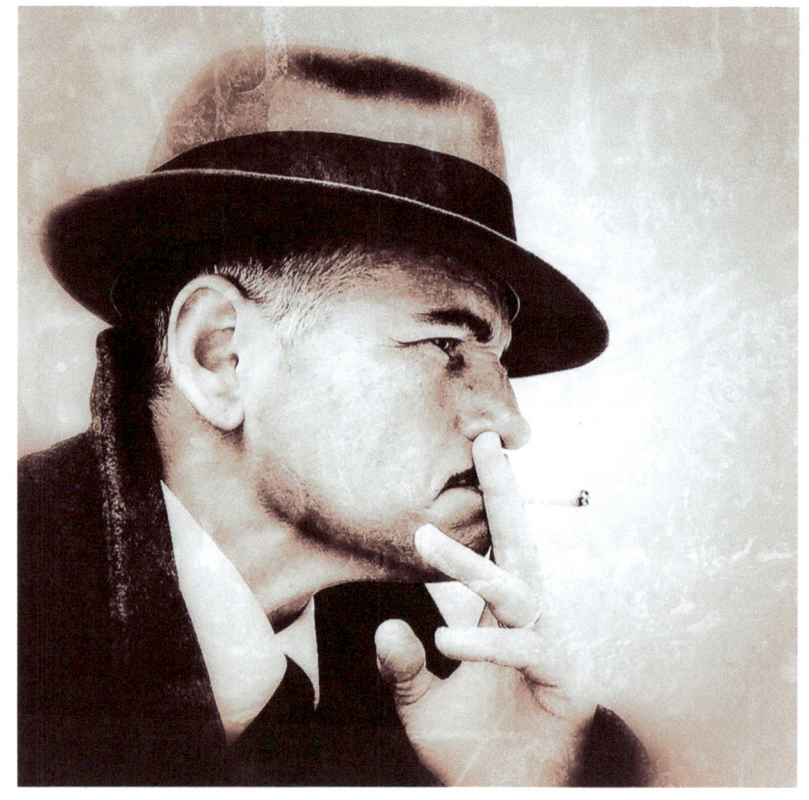

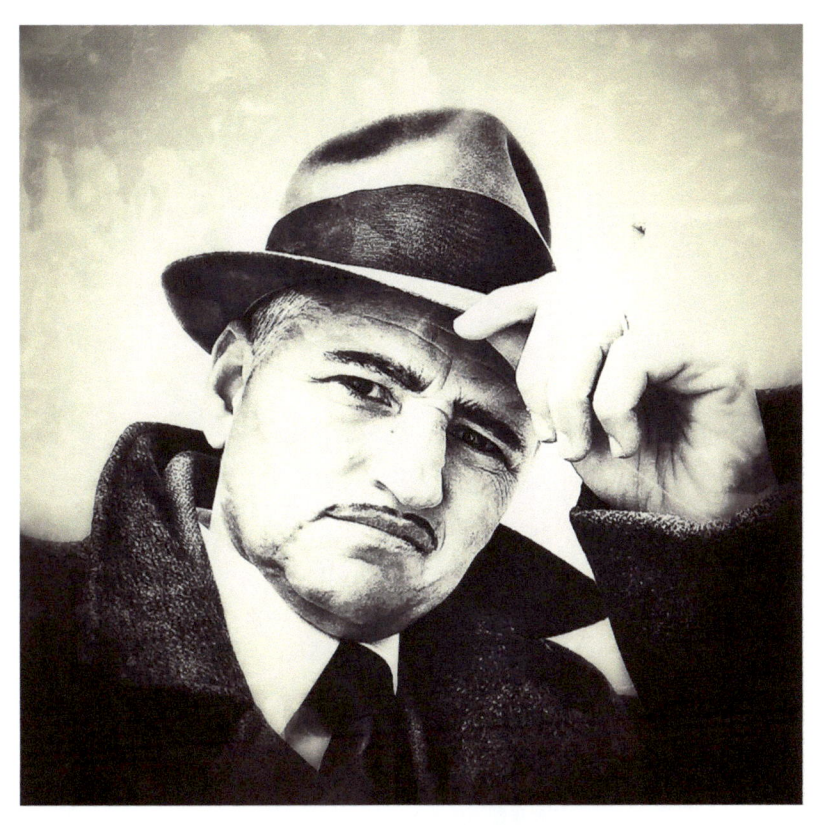

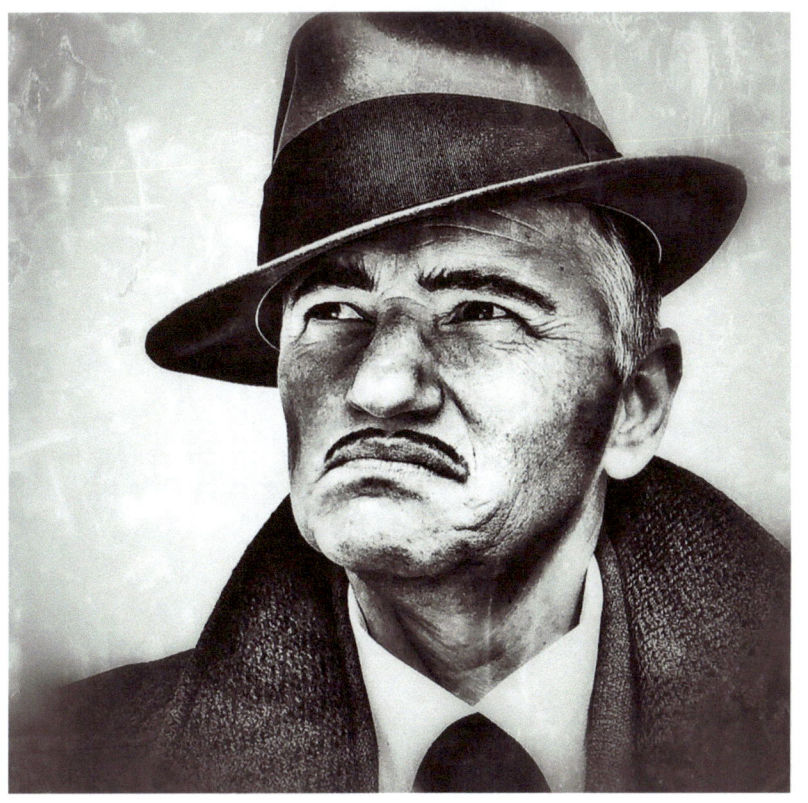

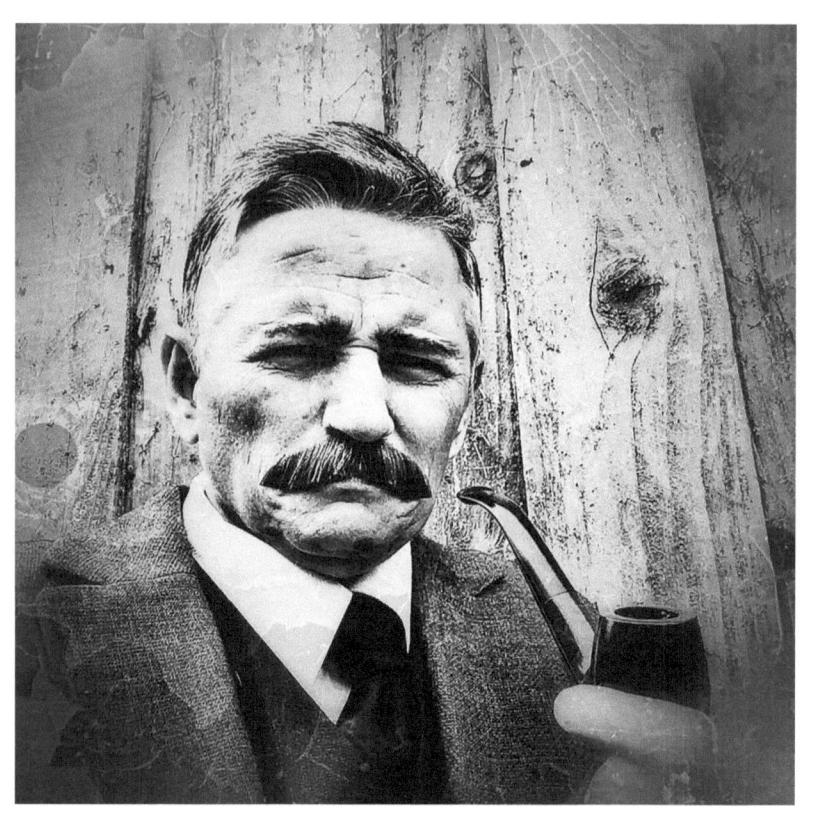

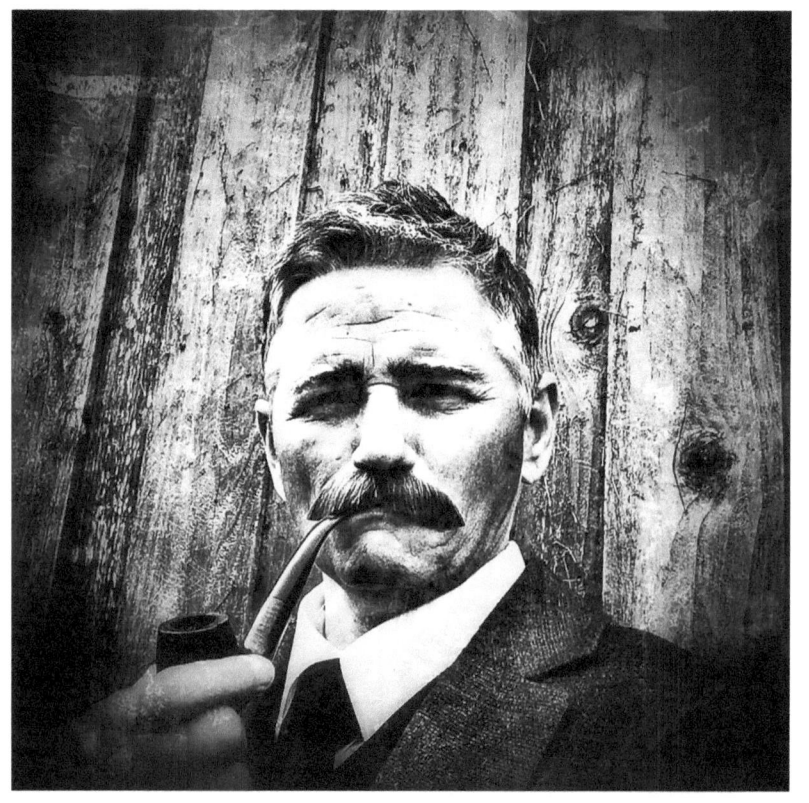

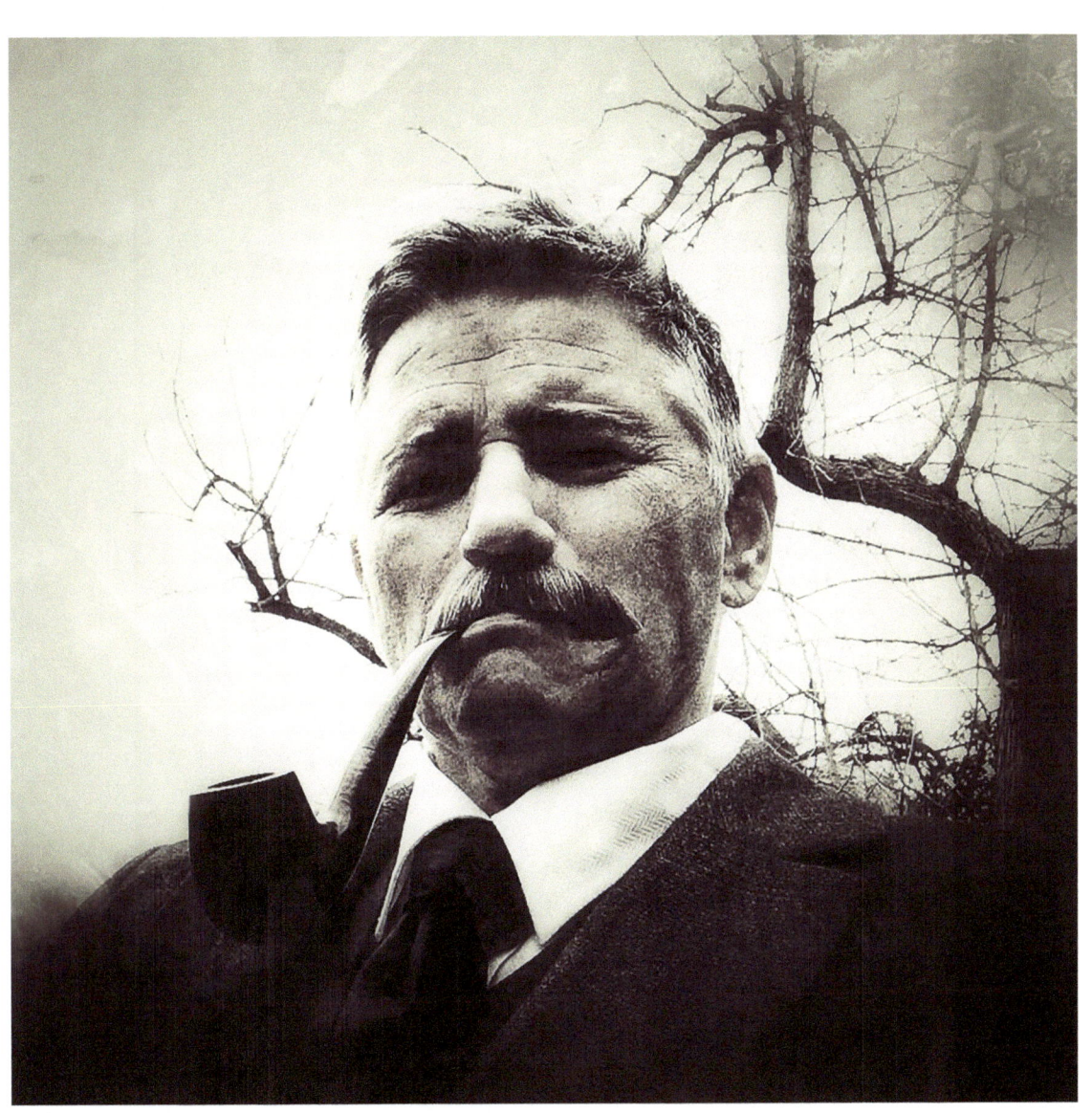

Francis Van der Lokey, III

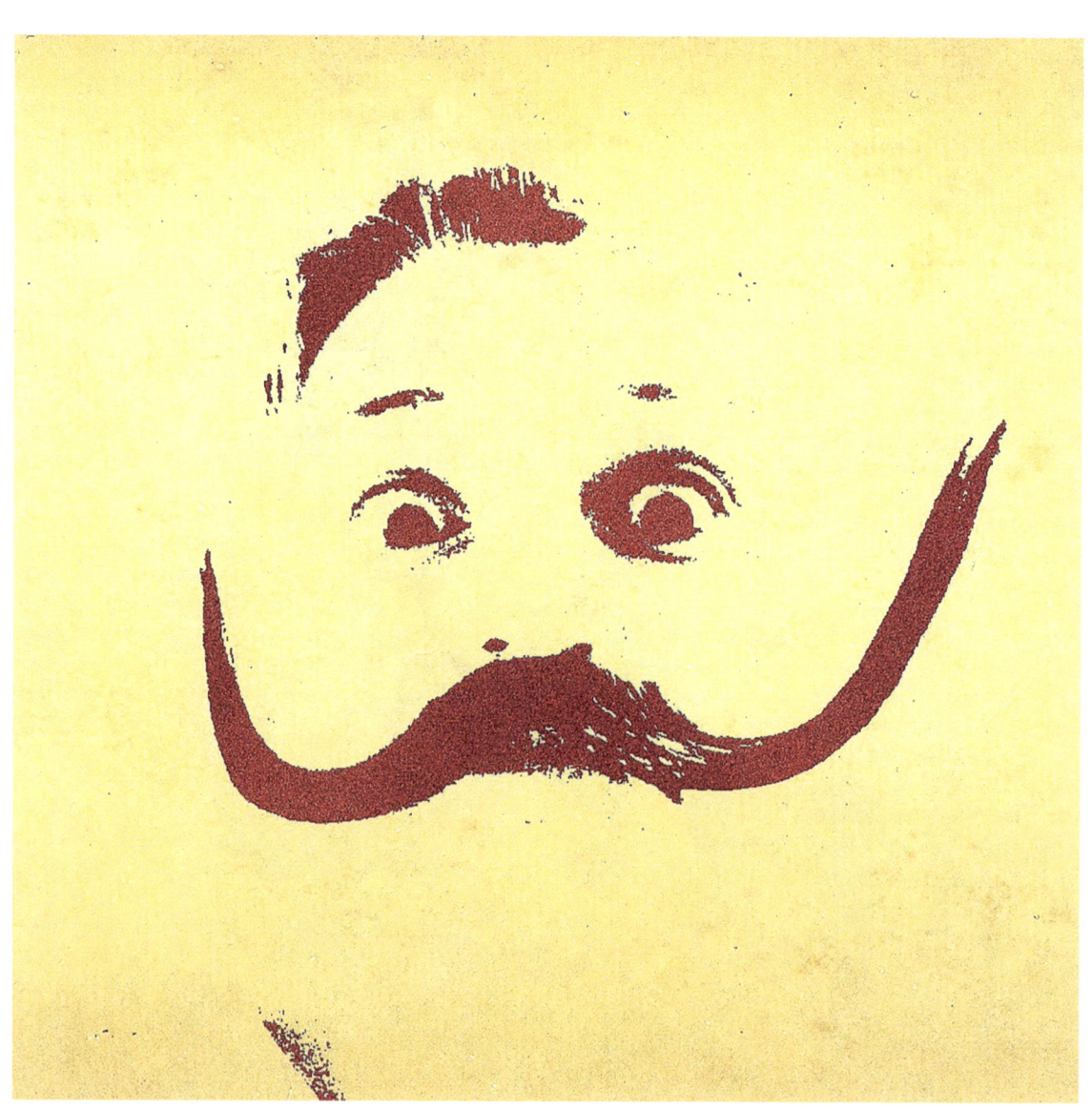

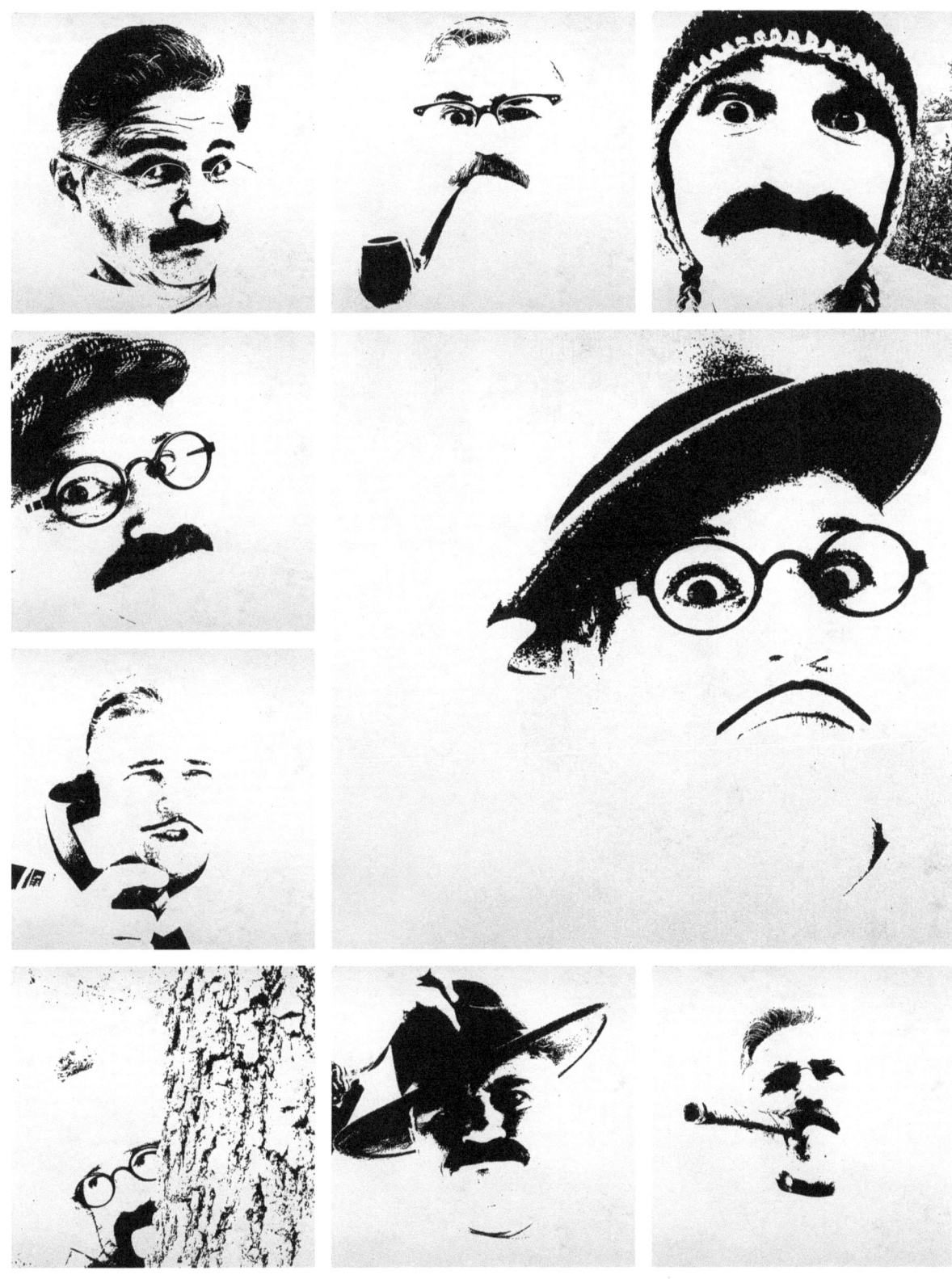

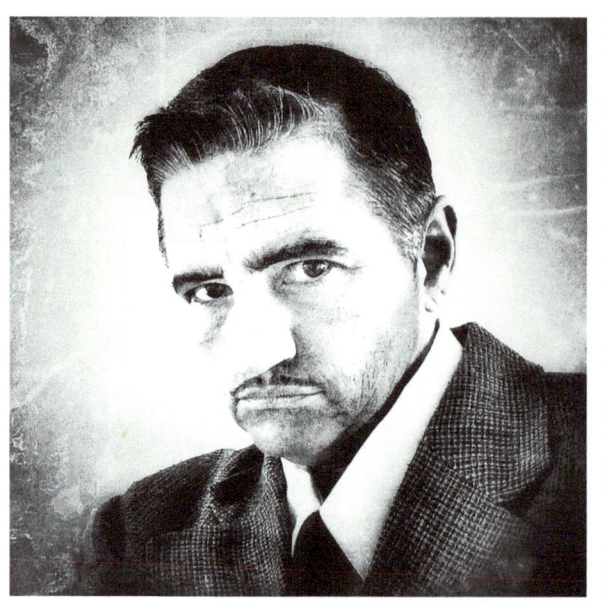
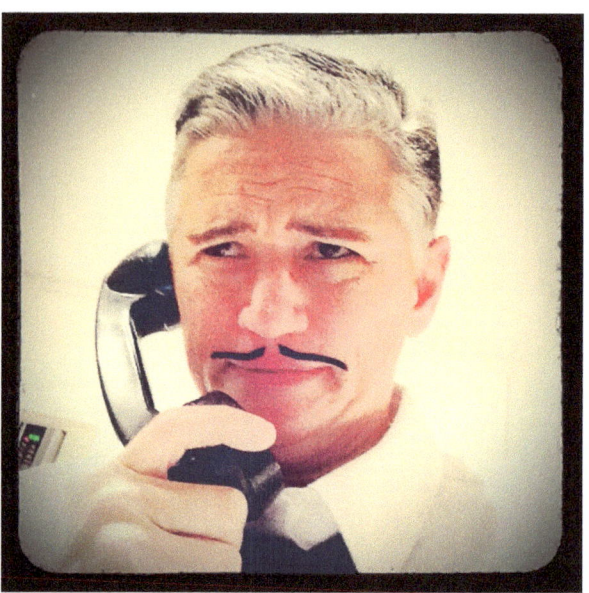
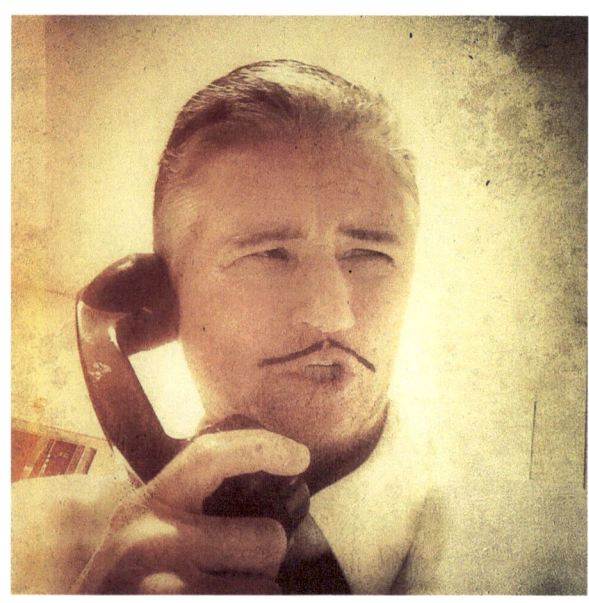
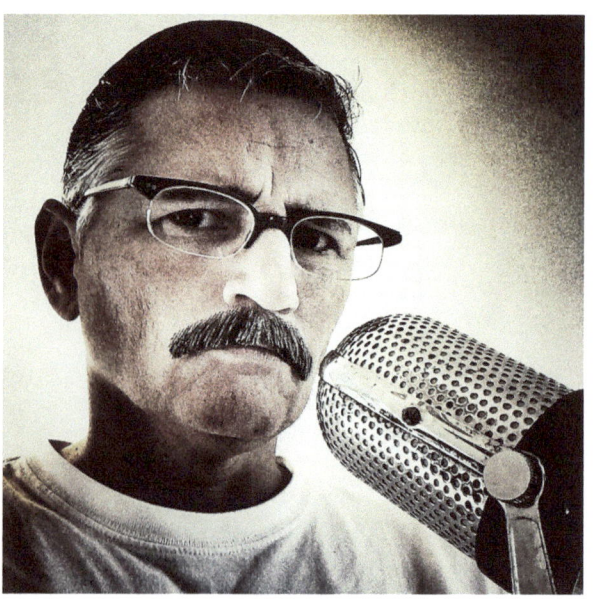

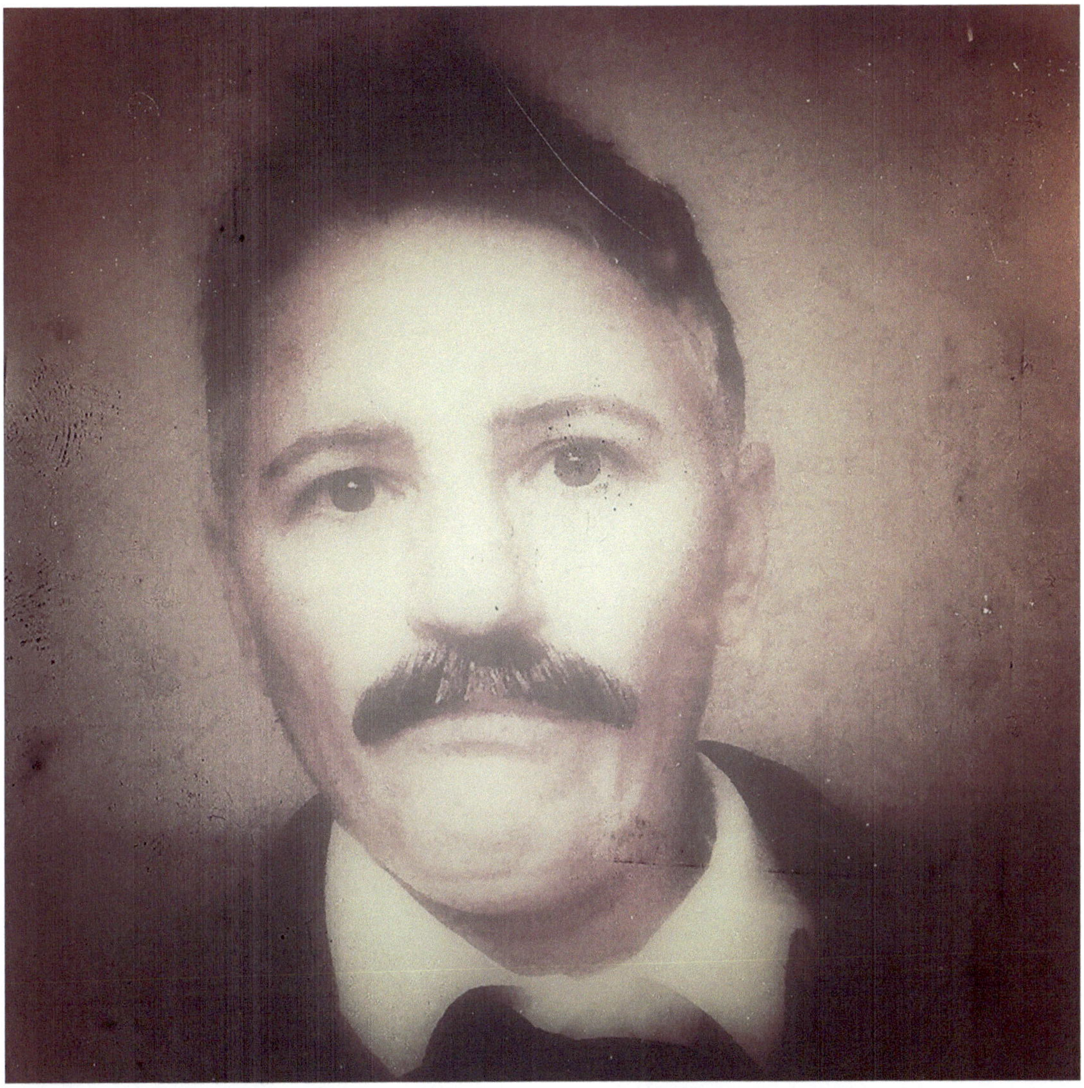

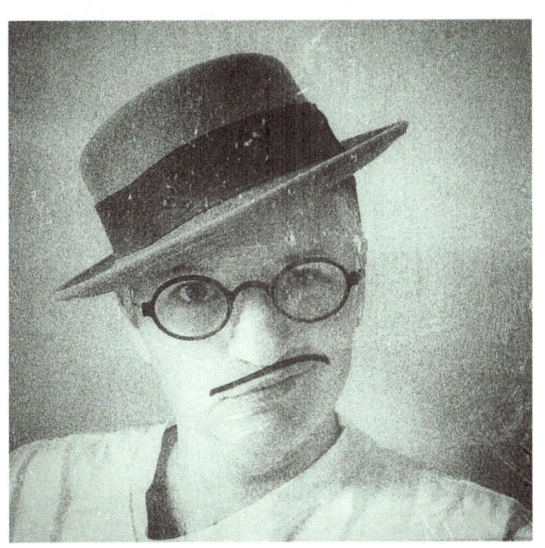
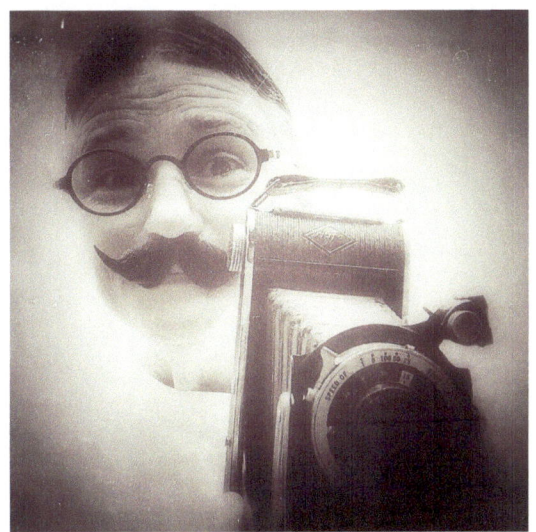

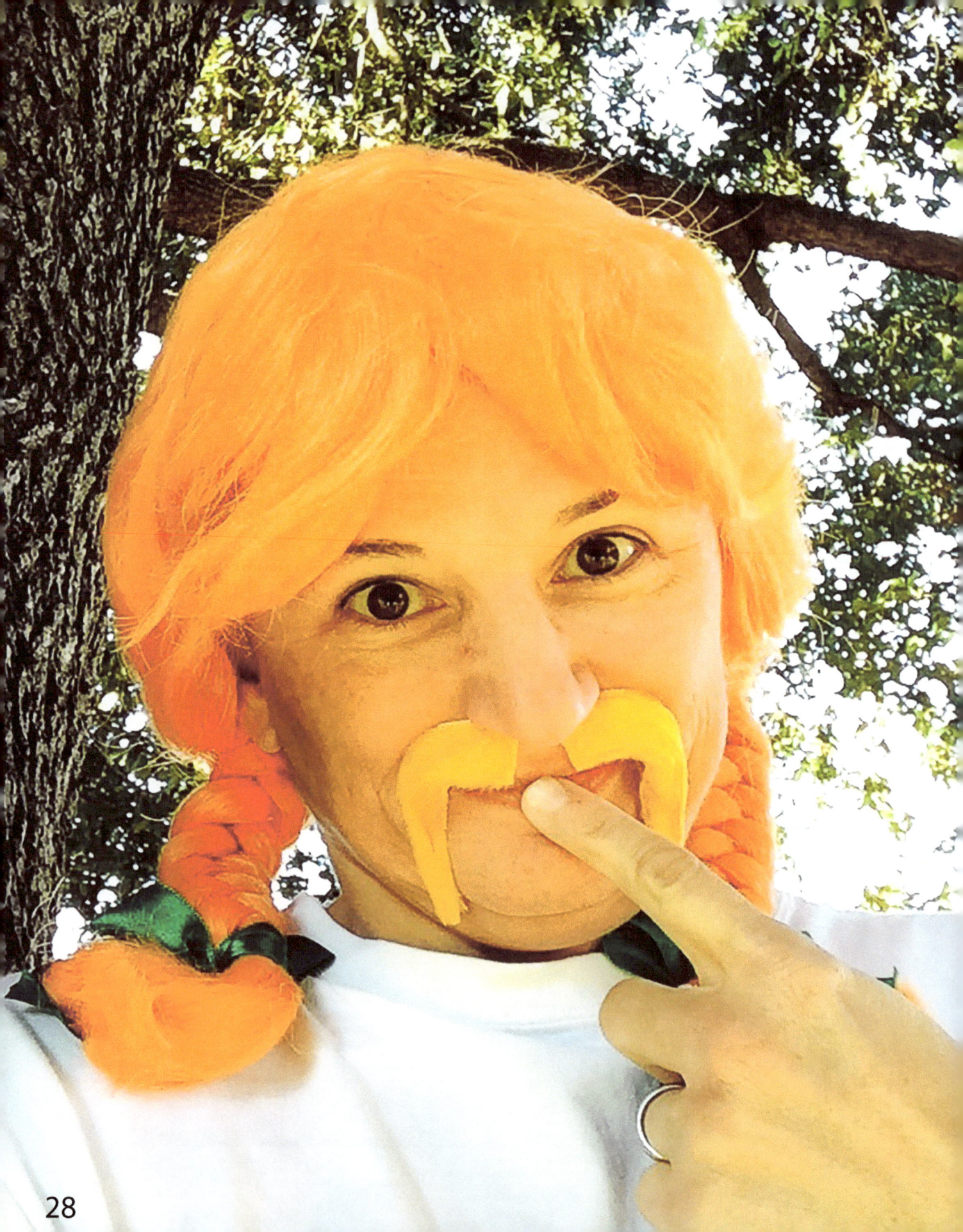

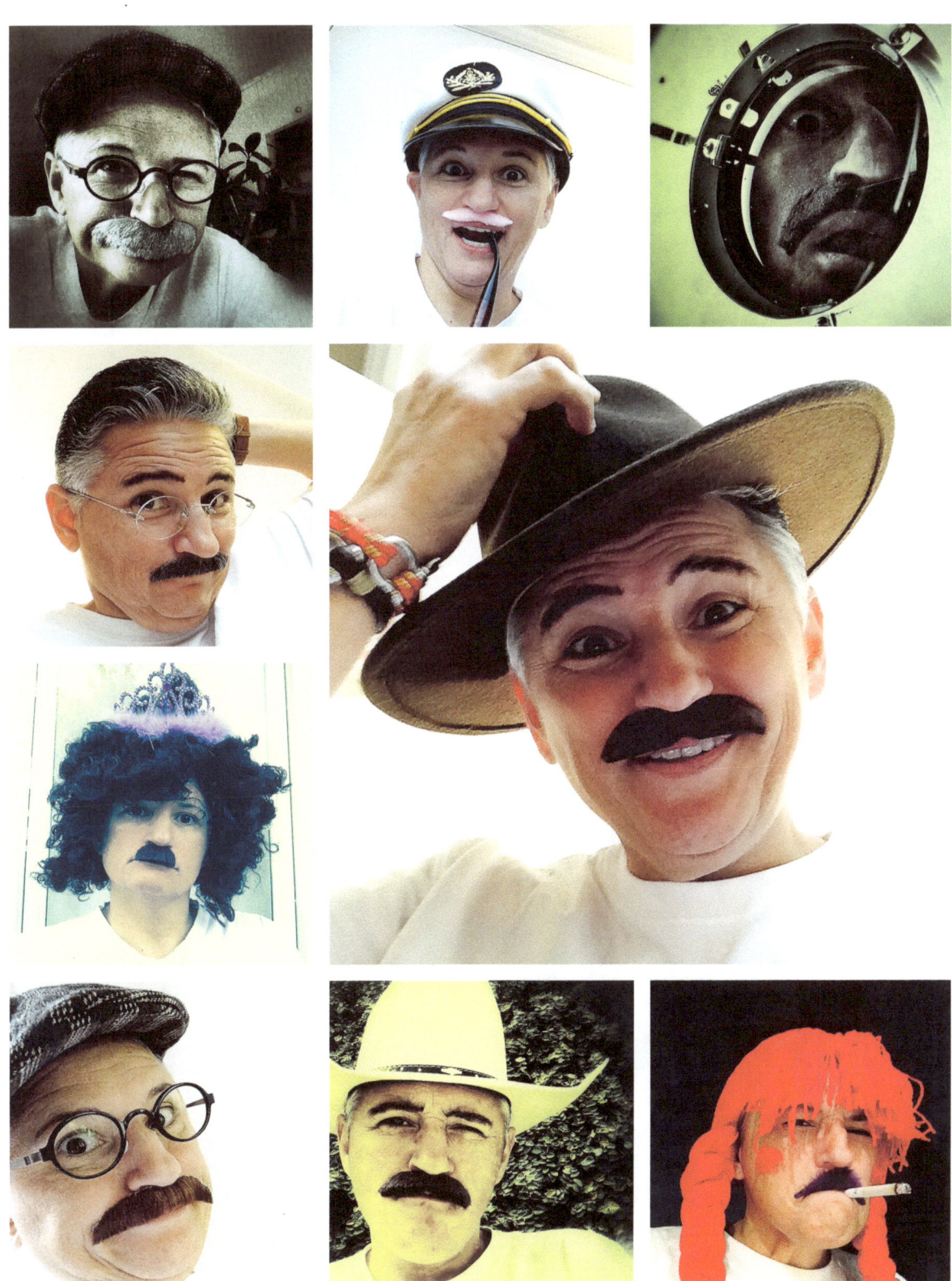

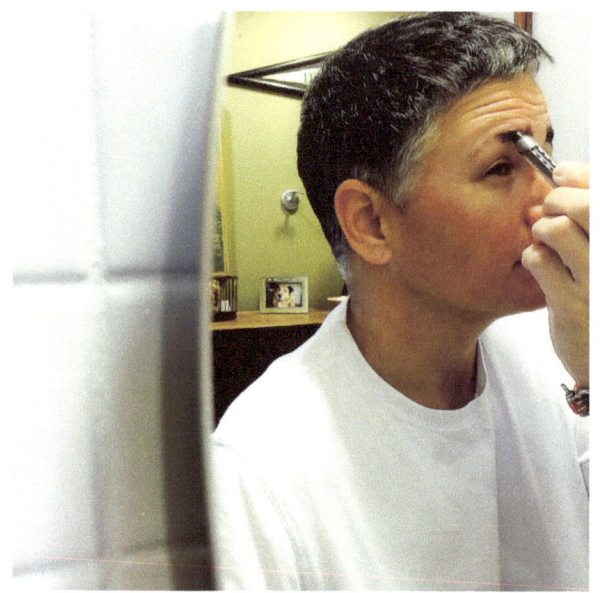
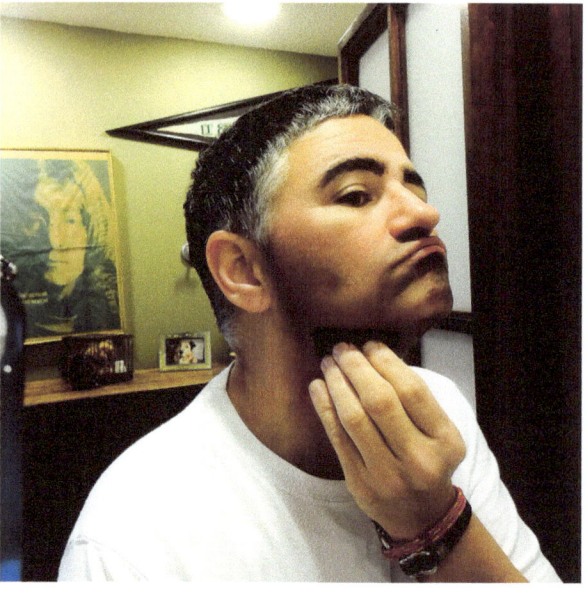

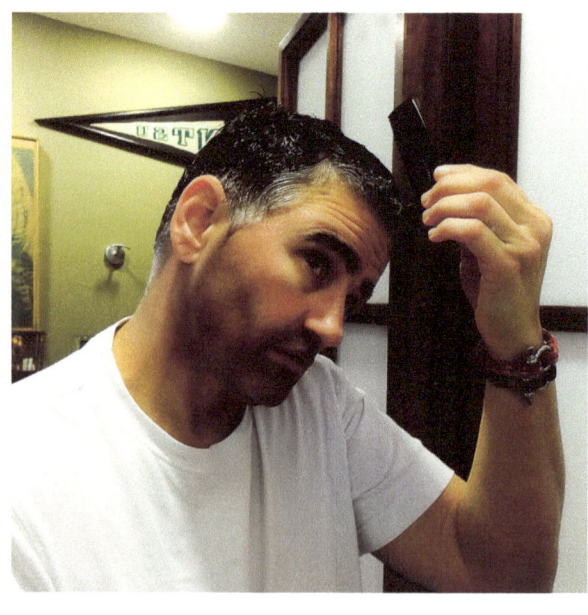
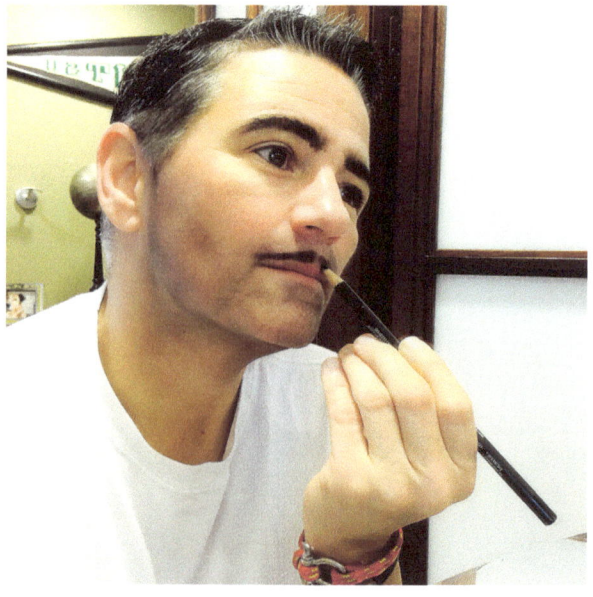

For most of the pictures, I used an eyebrow pencil for the eyebrows and smaller moustaches and face paint for the five o'clock shadow. And lots of hair gel.

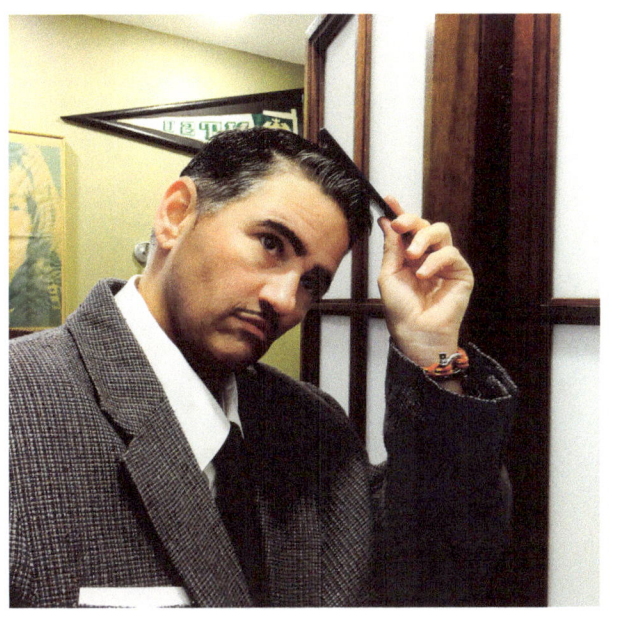

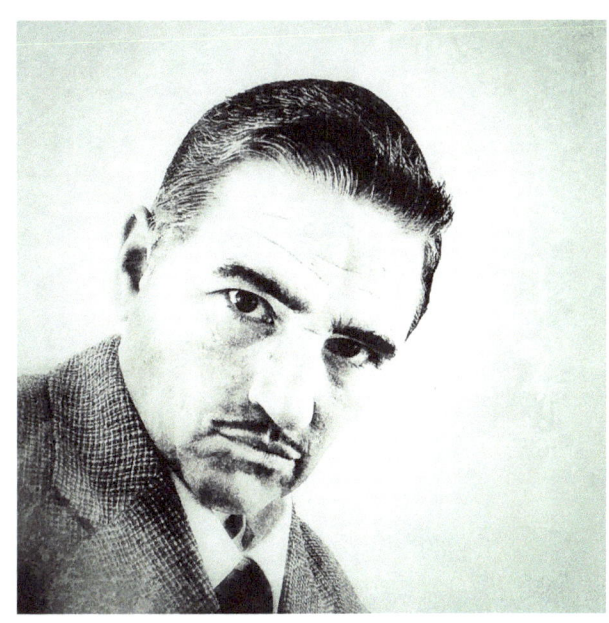

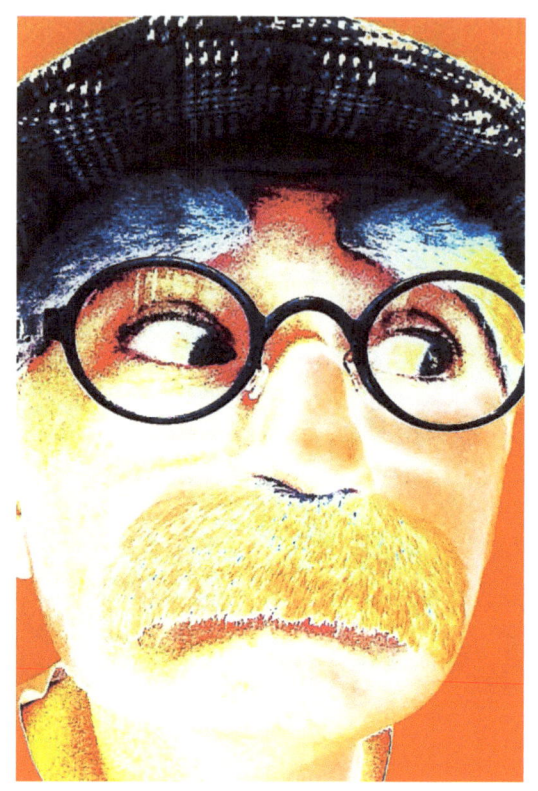
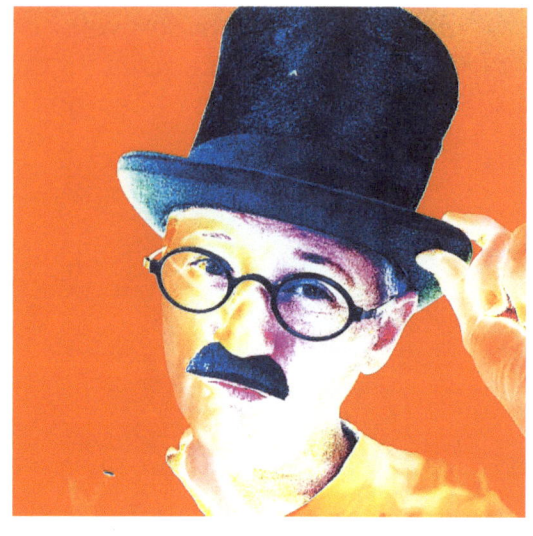
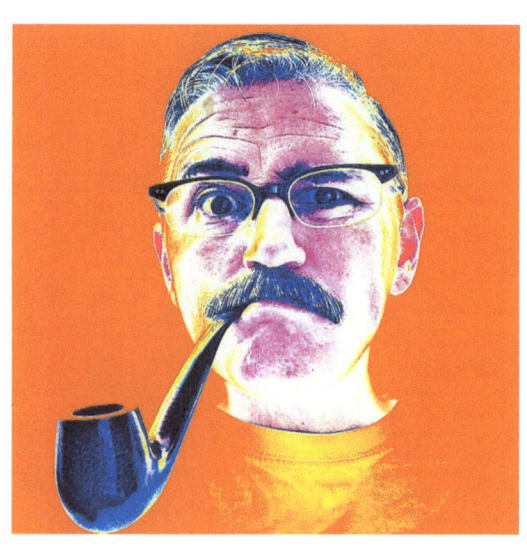
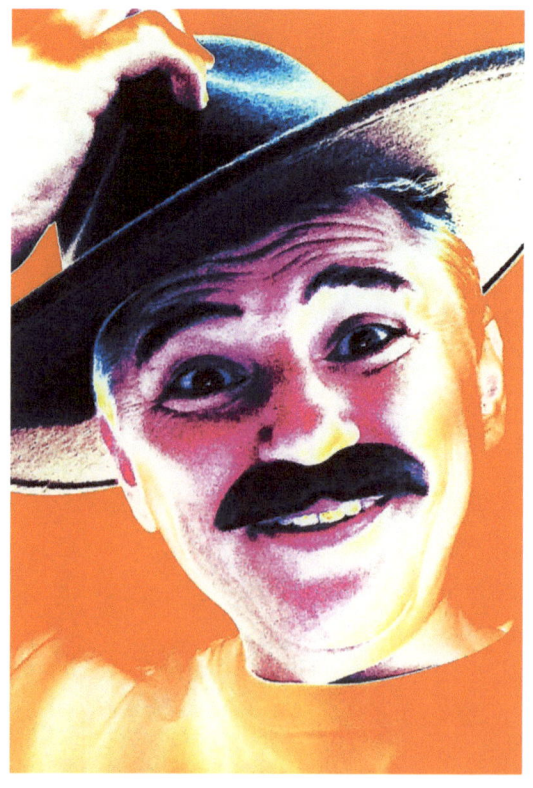

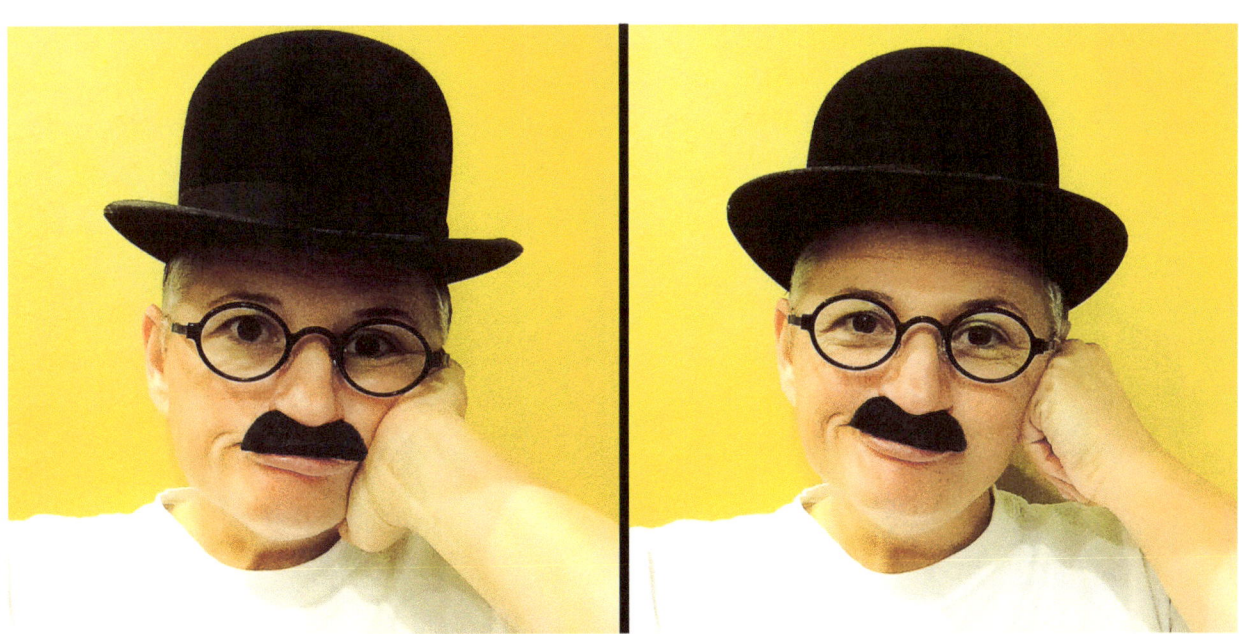

One's willingness to look ridiculous on camera is key in becoming a good subject. I have taken some pictures of myself and said, "I should not post this; it is crazy" as I hit the post button. Strangely, becoming other characters has made me more comfortable with myself; I do not dwell on my "imperfections" as much as I did in the past. Everyone is a character; we should embrace our uniqueness.

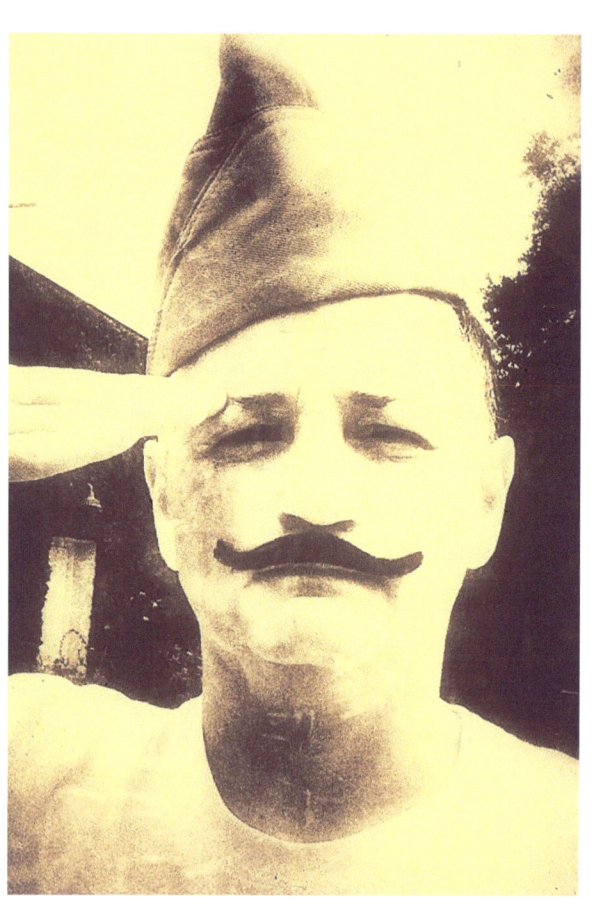

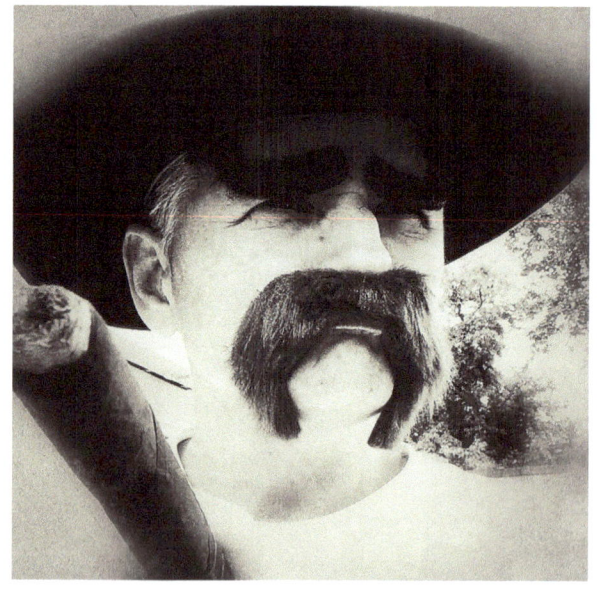

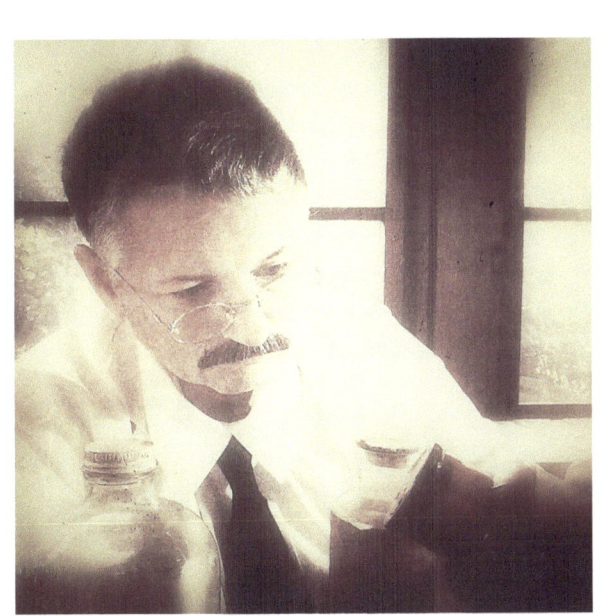
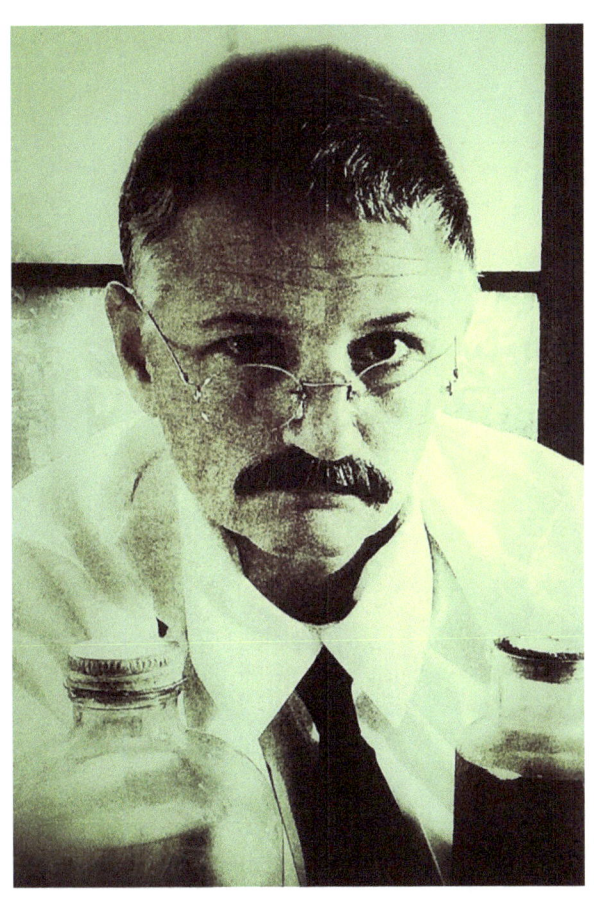

Dr. Granville Van der Lokey, III

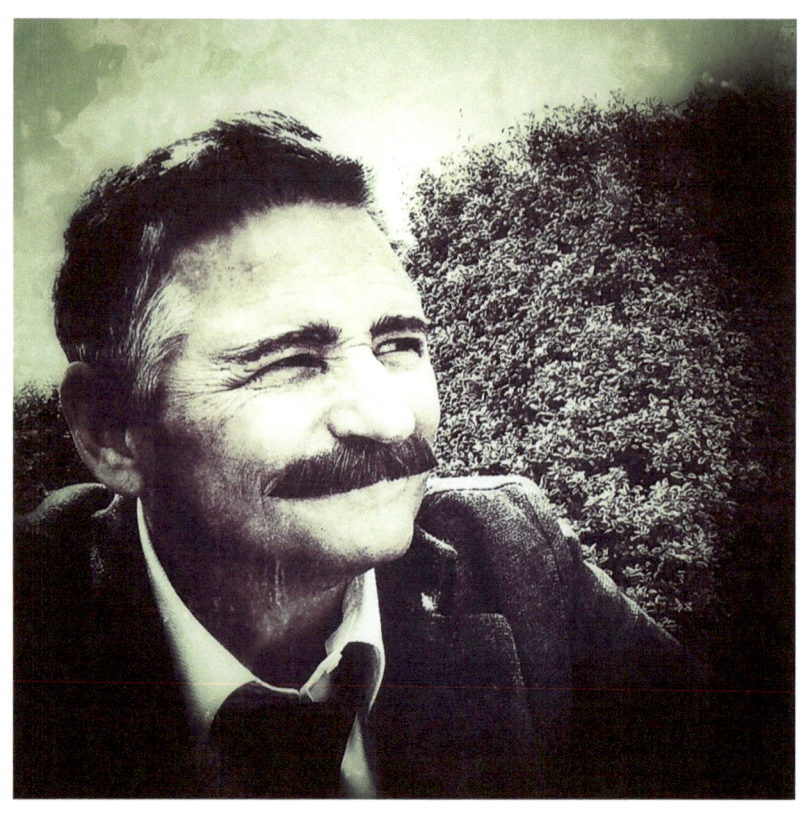

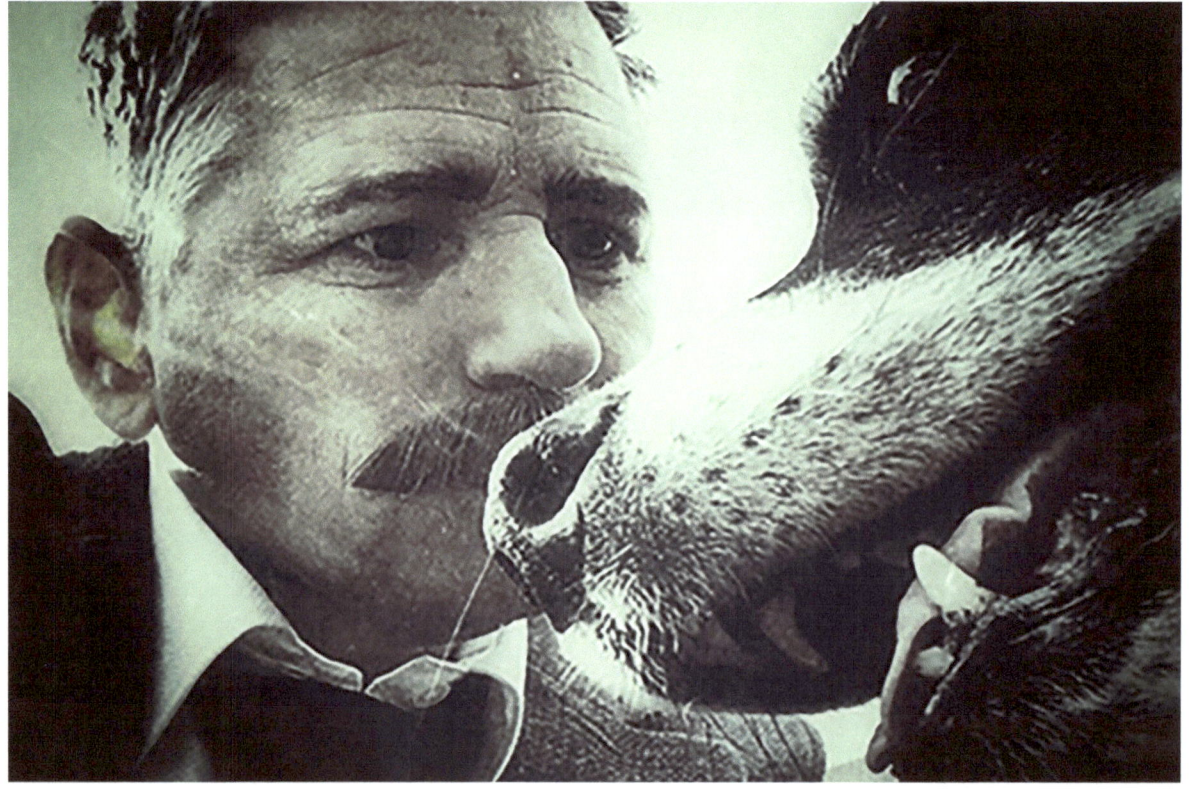

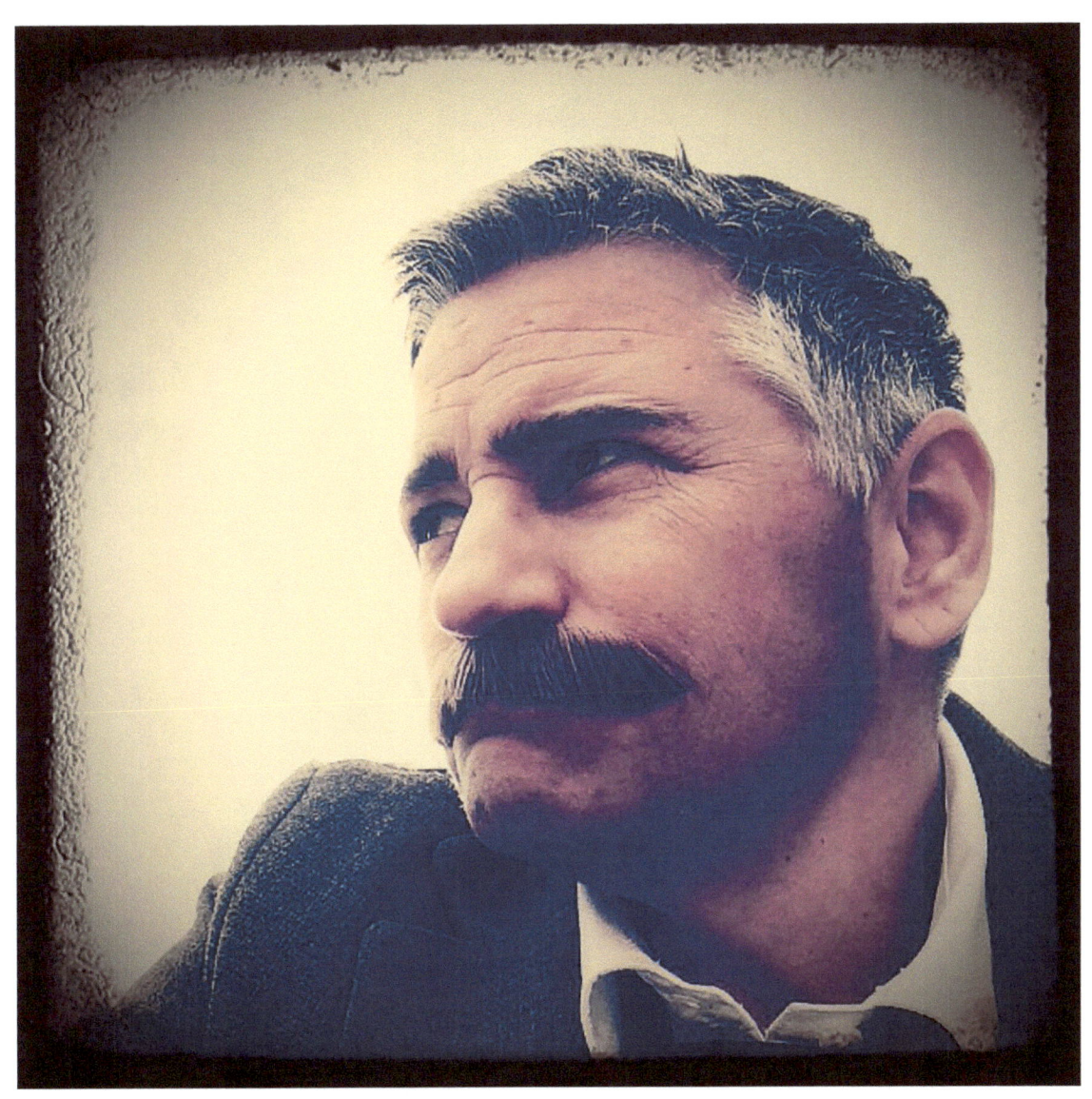

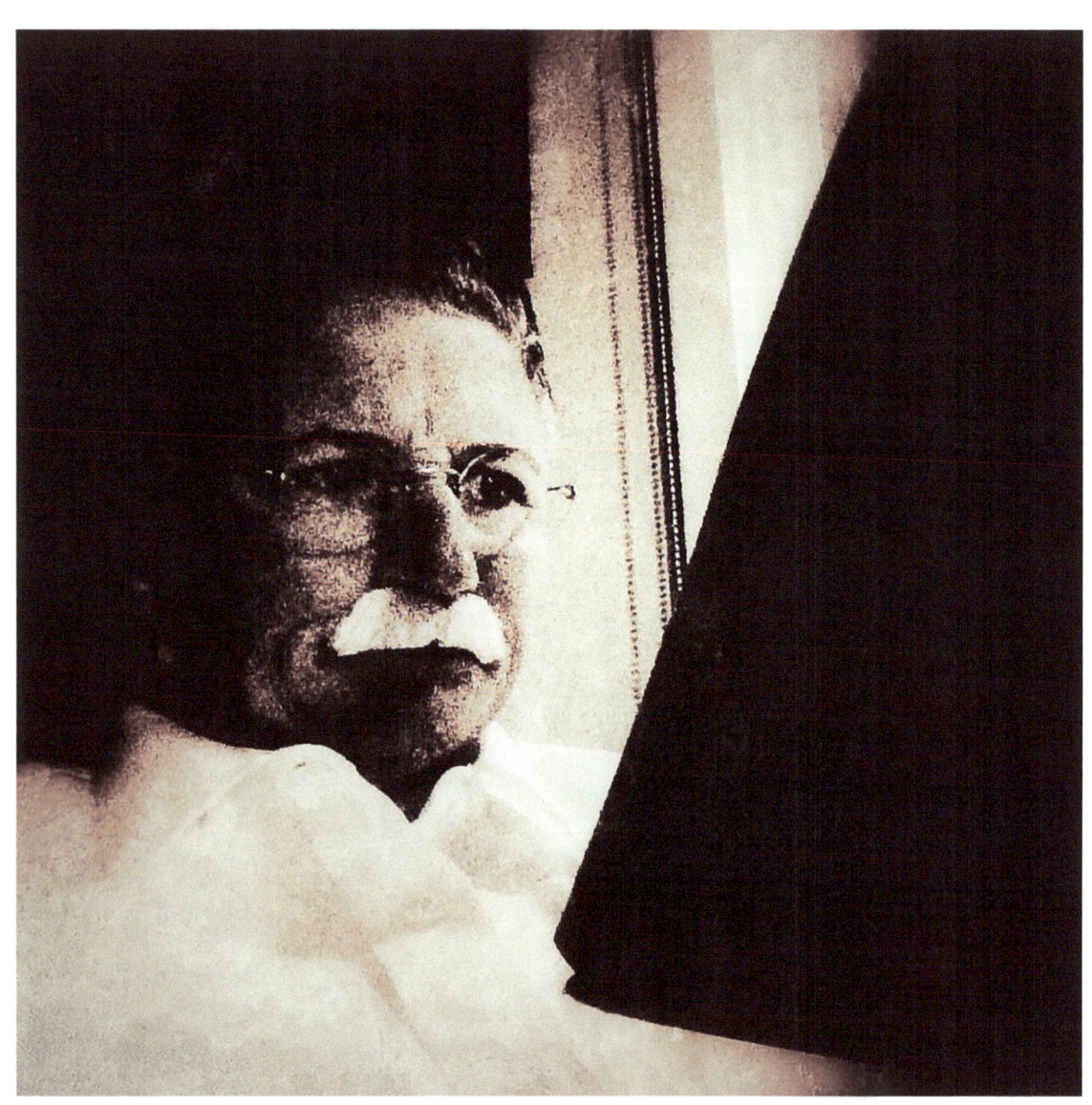

Grandpa Van der Lokey, III

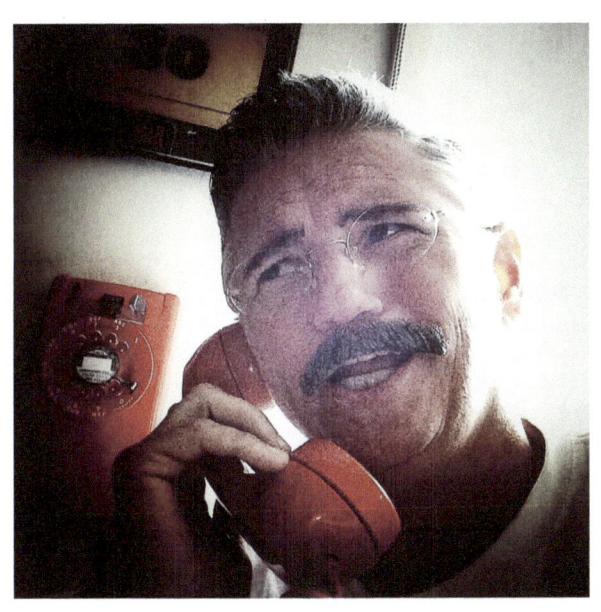 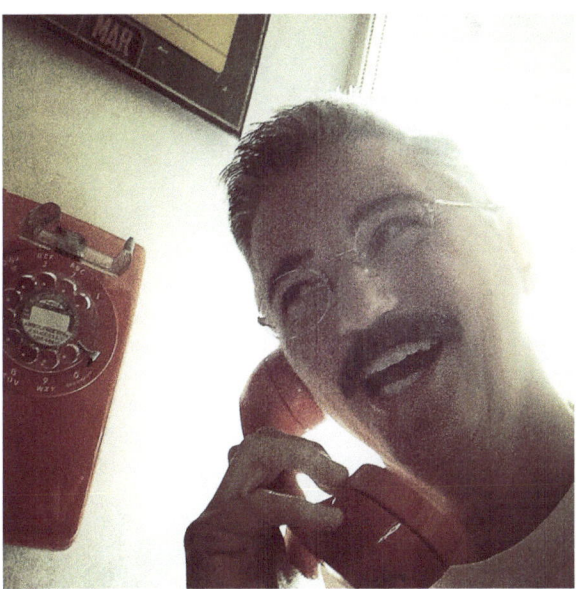

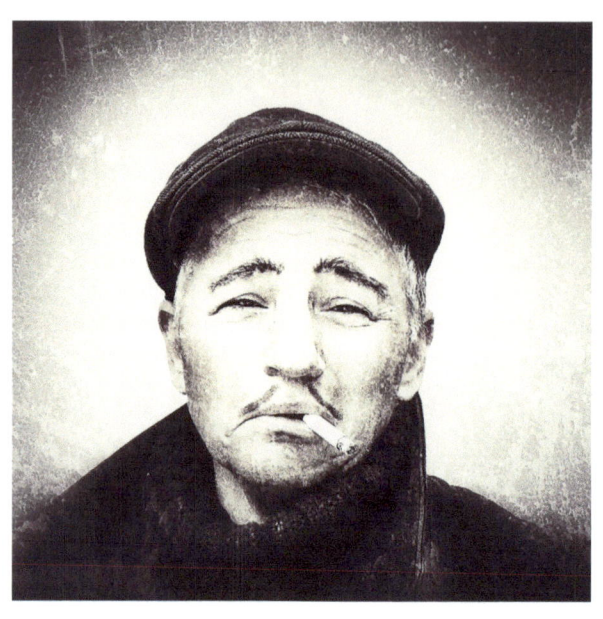
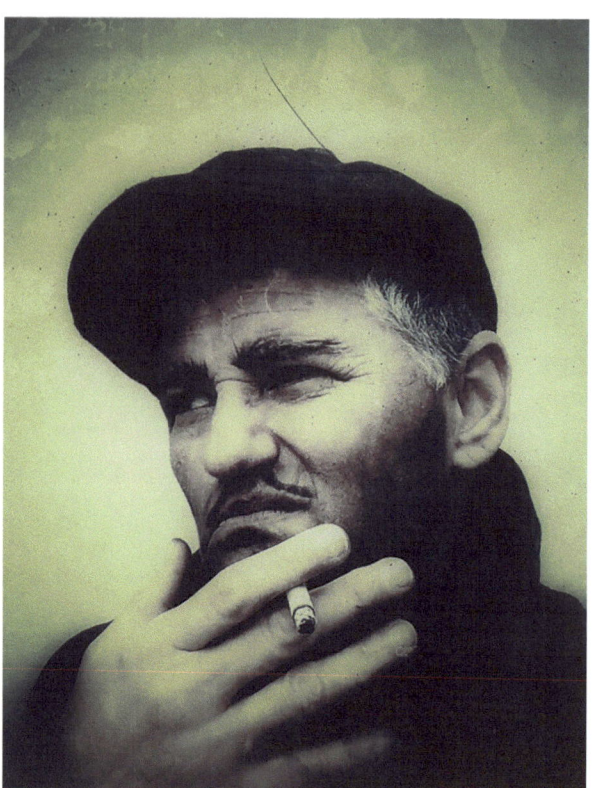
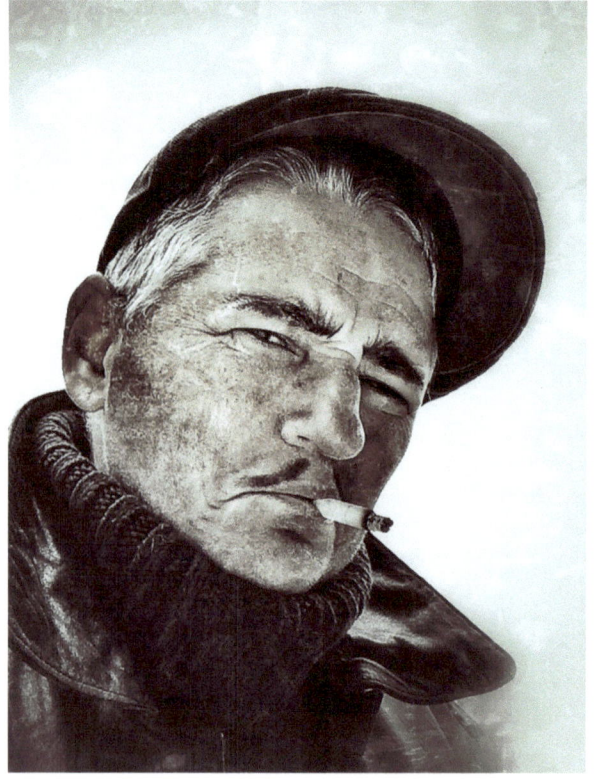
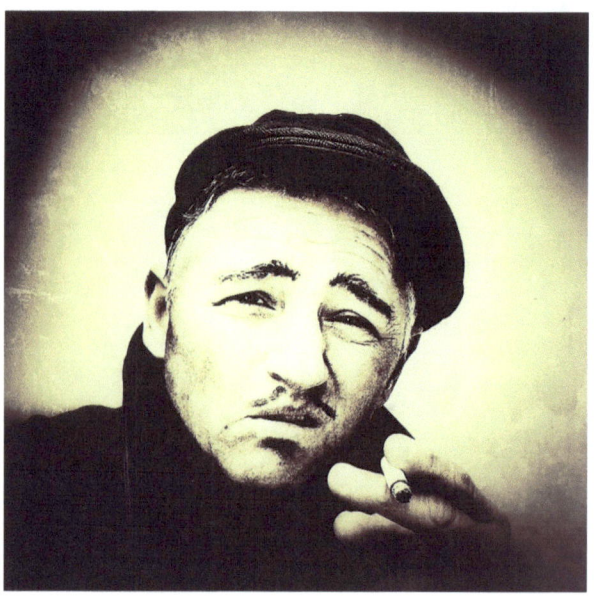

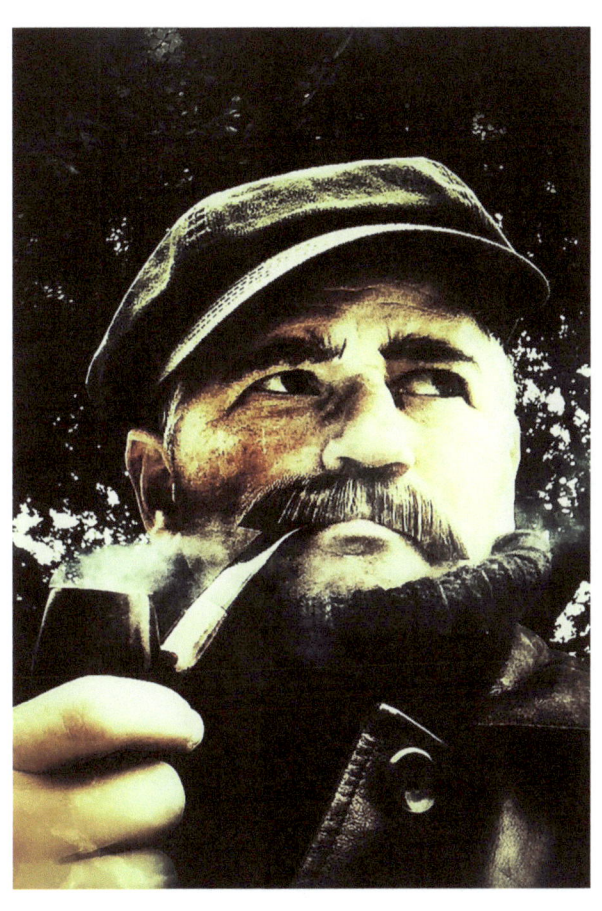

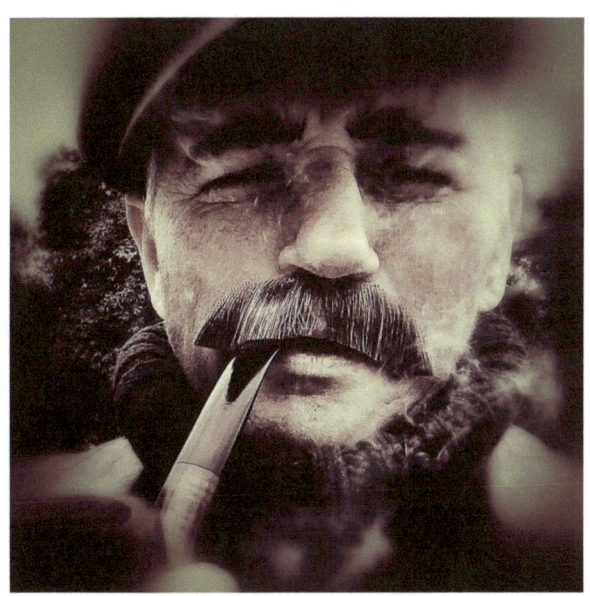

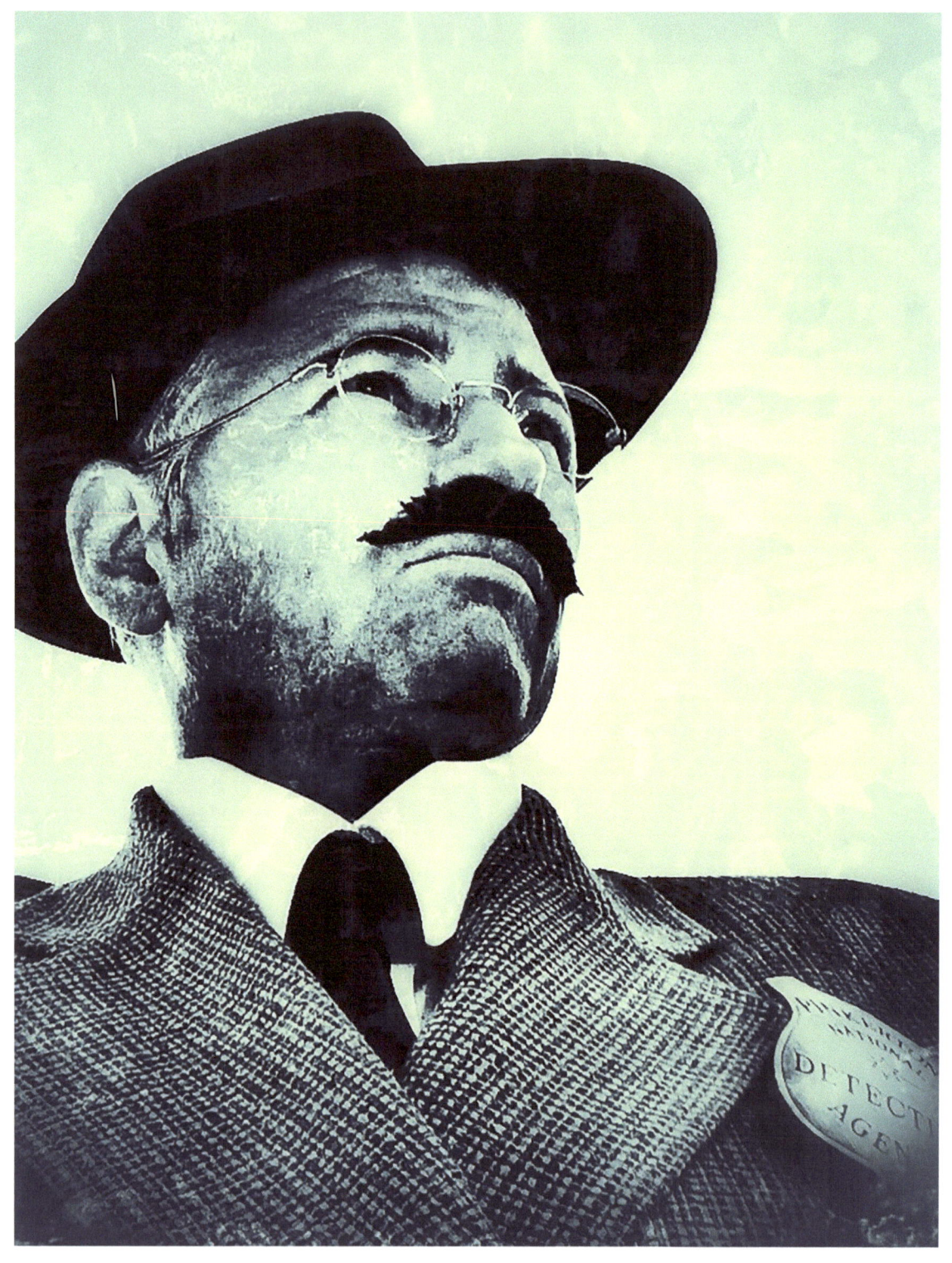

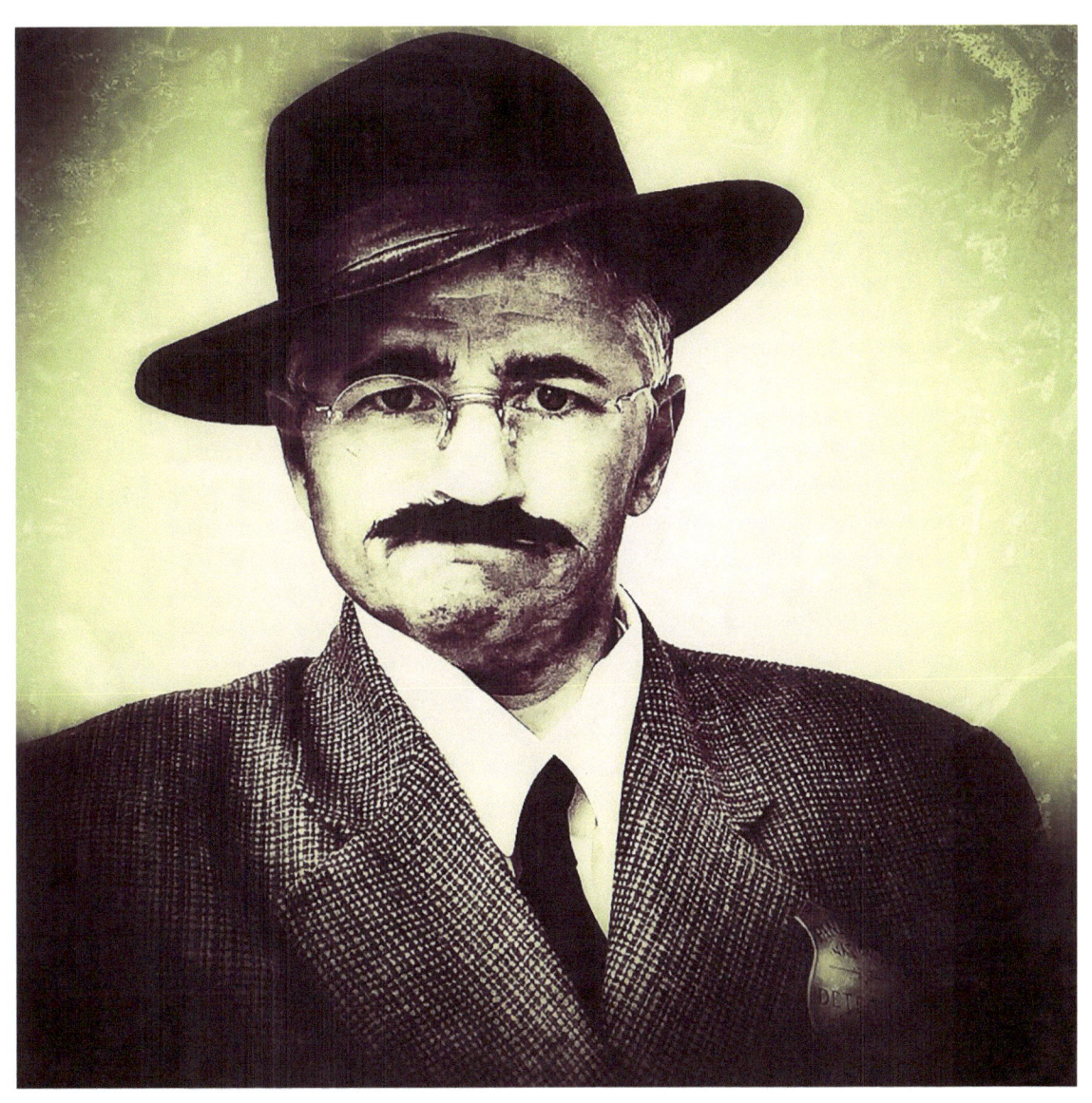

Elliott N. Van der Lokey, III

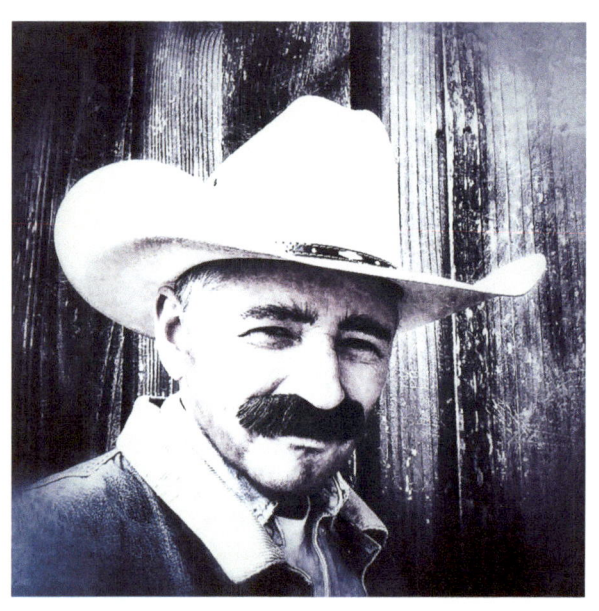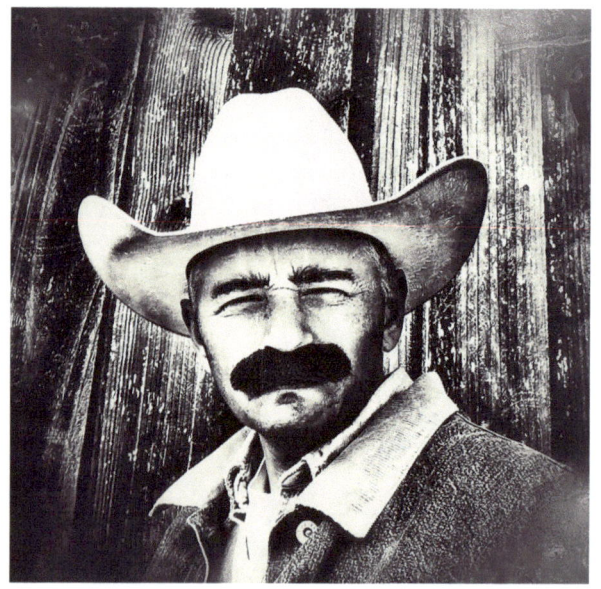

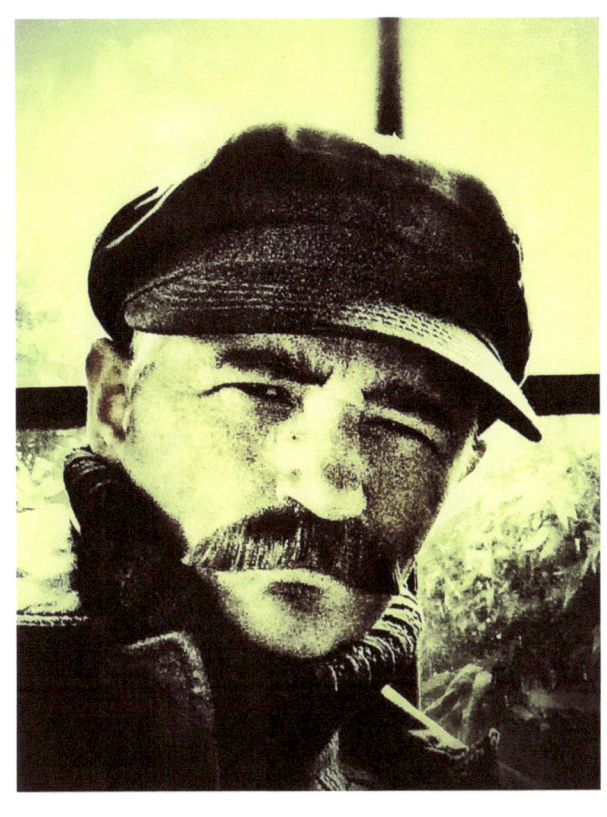
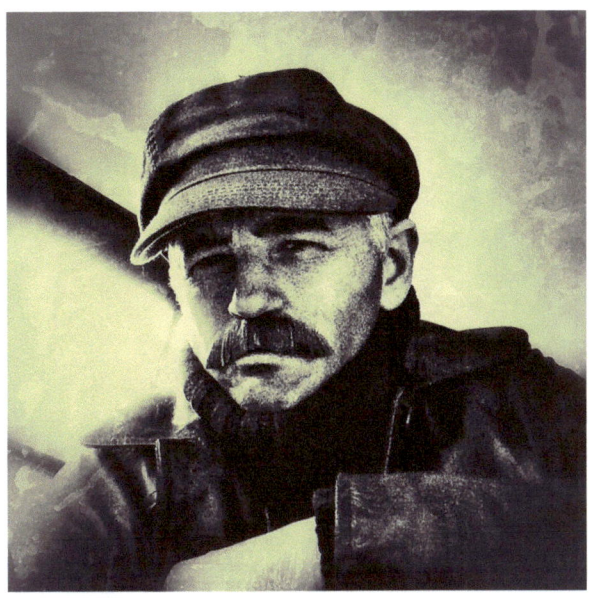
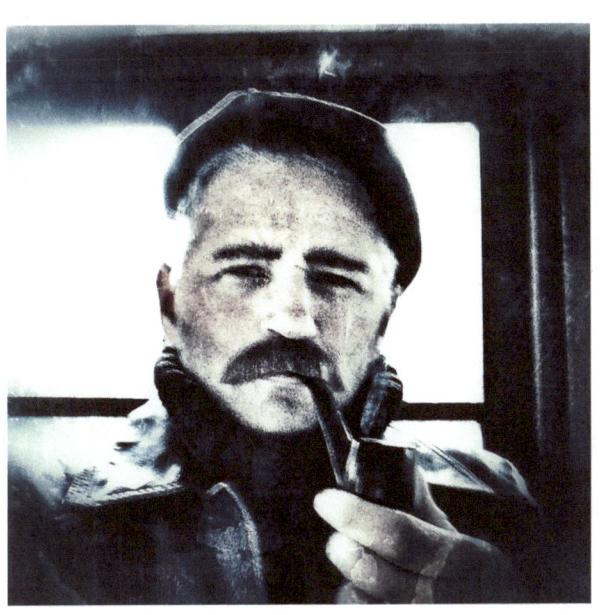
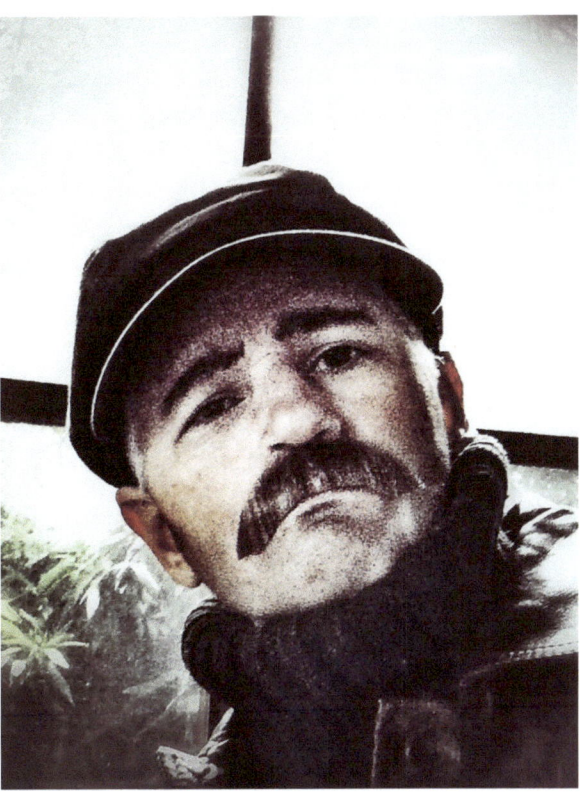

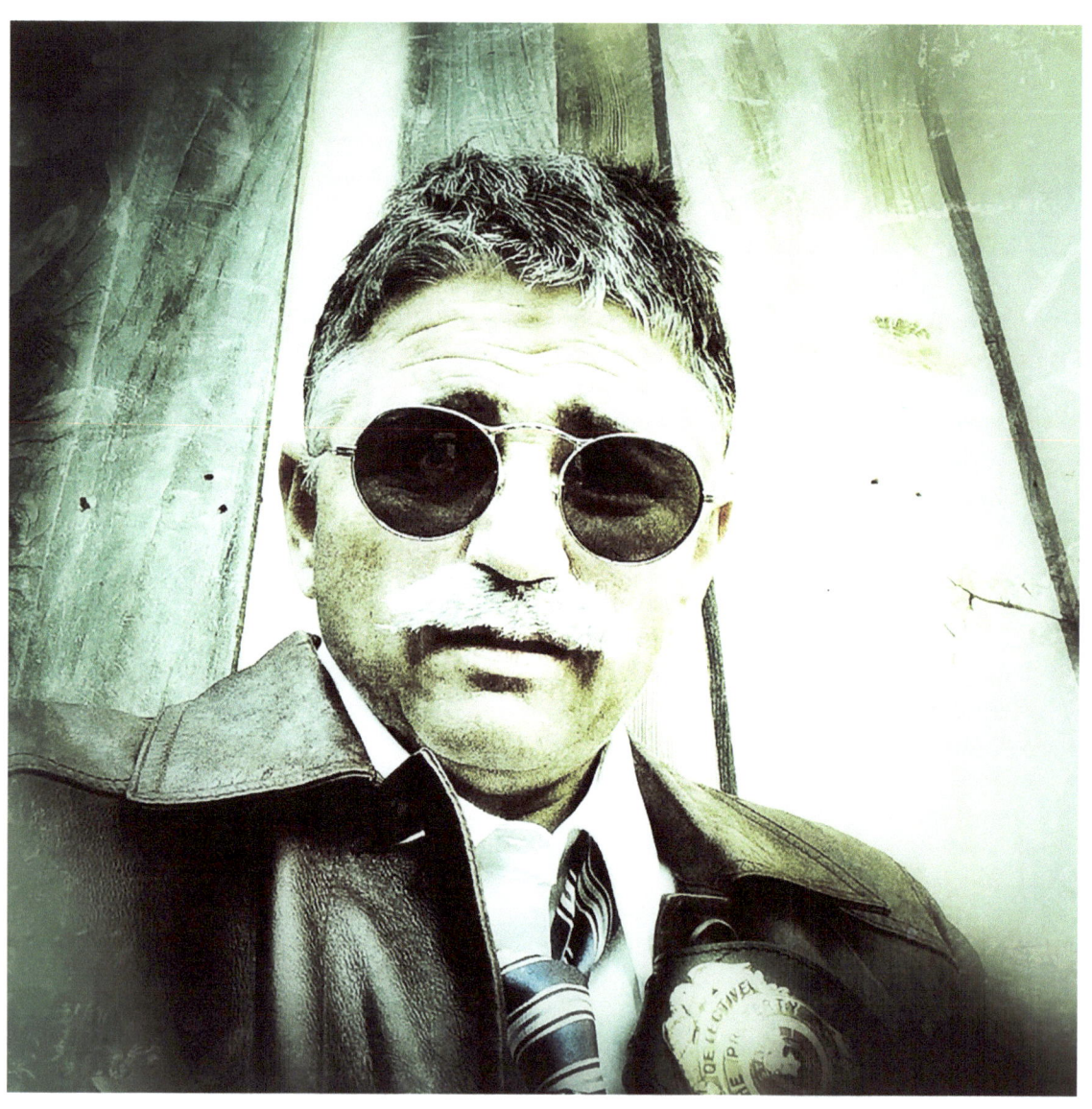

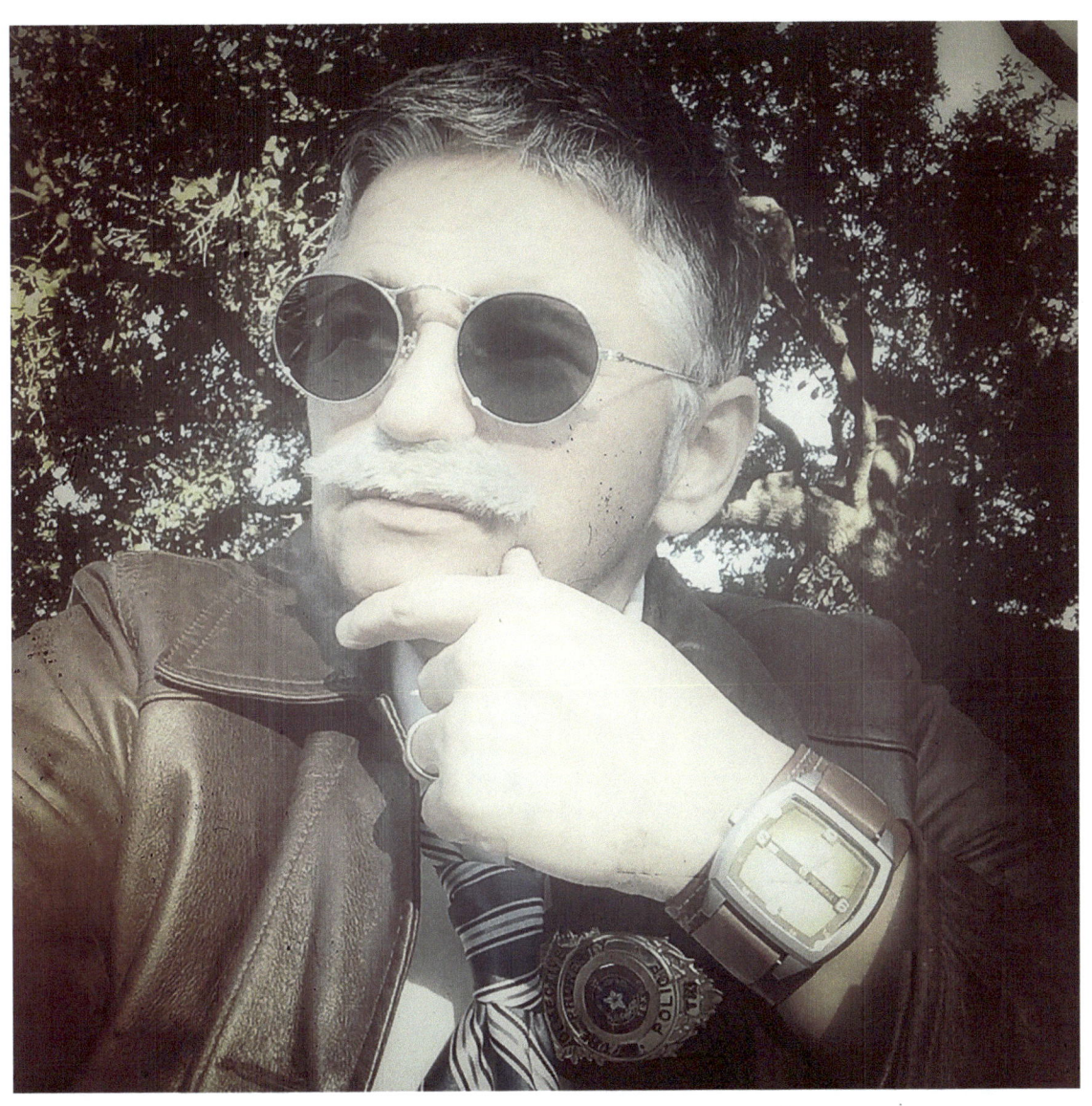

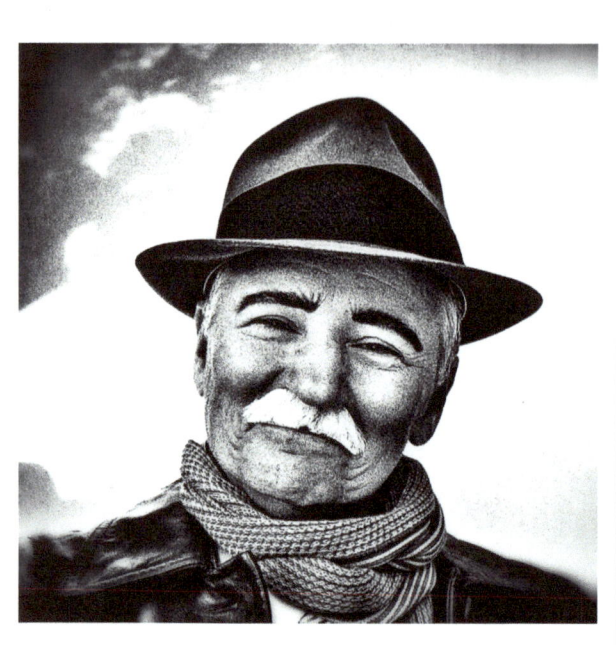

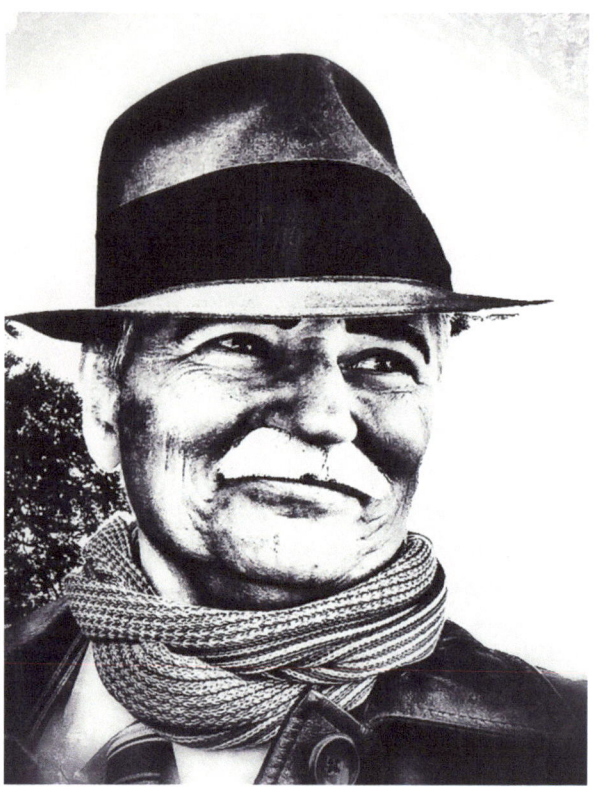

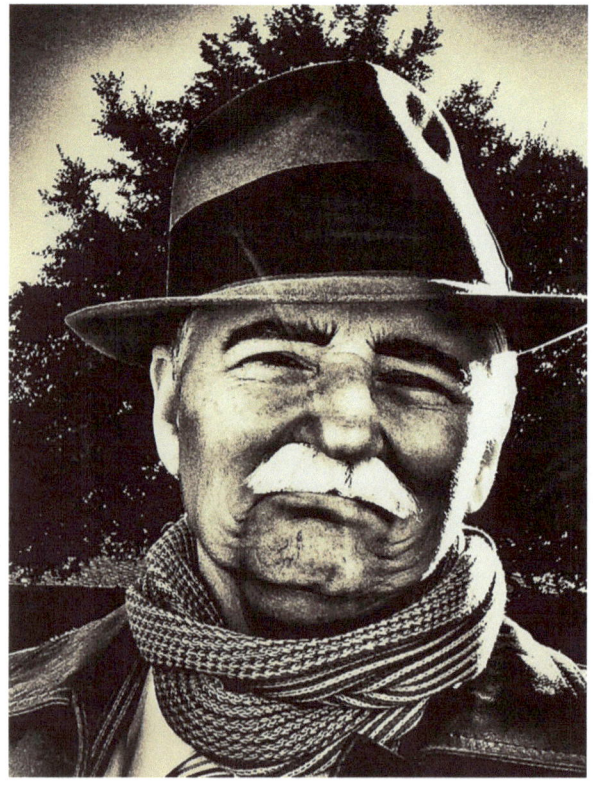

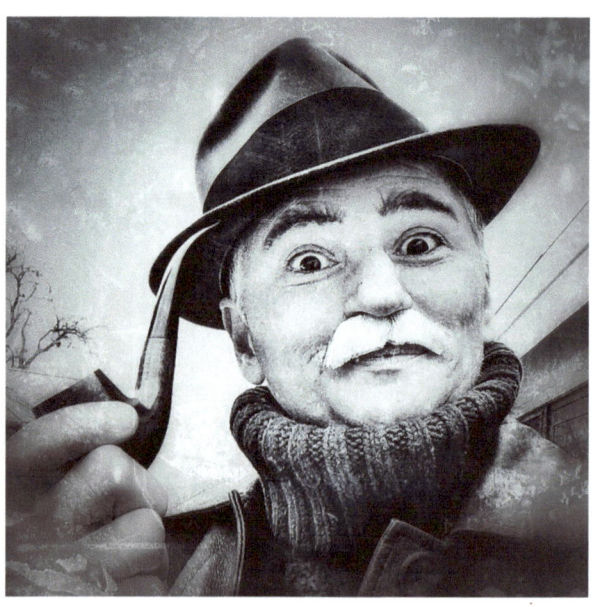

48

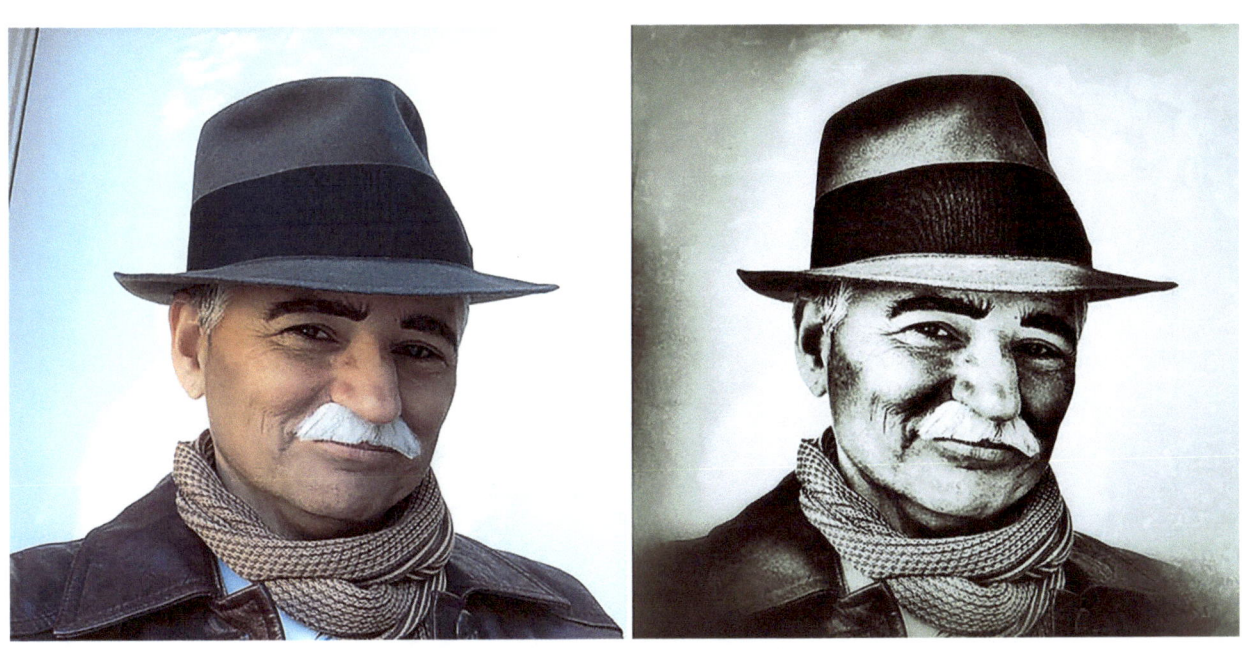

This was one of the pictures in which I did not recognize myself, and even though that became the goal of this project; it surprised me, nonetheless.

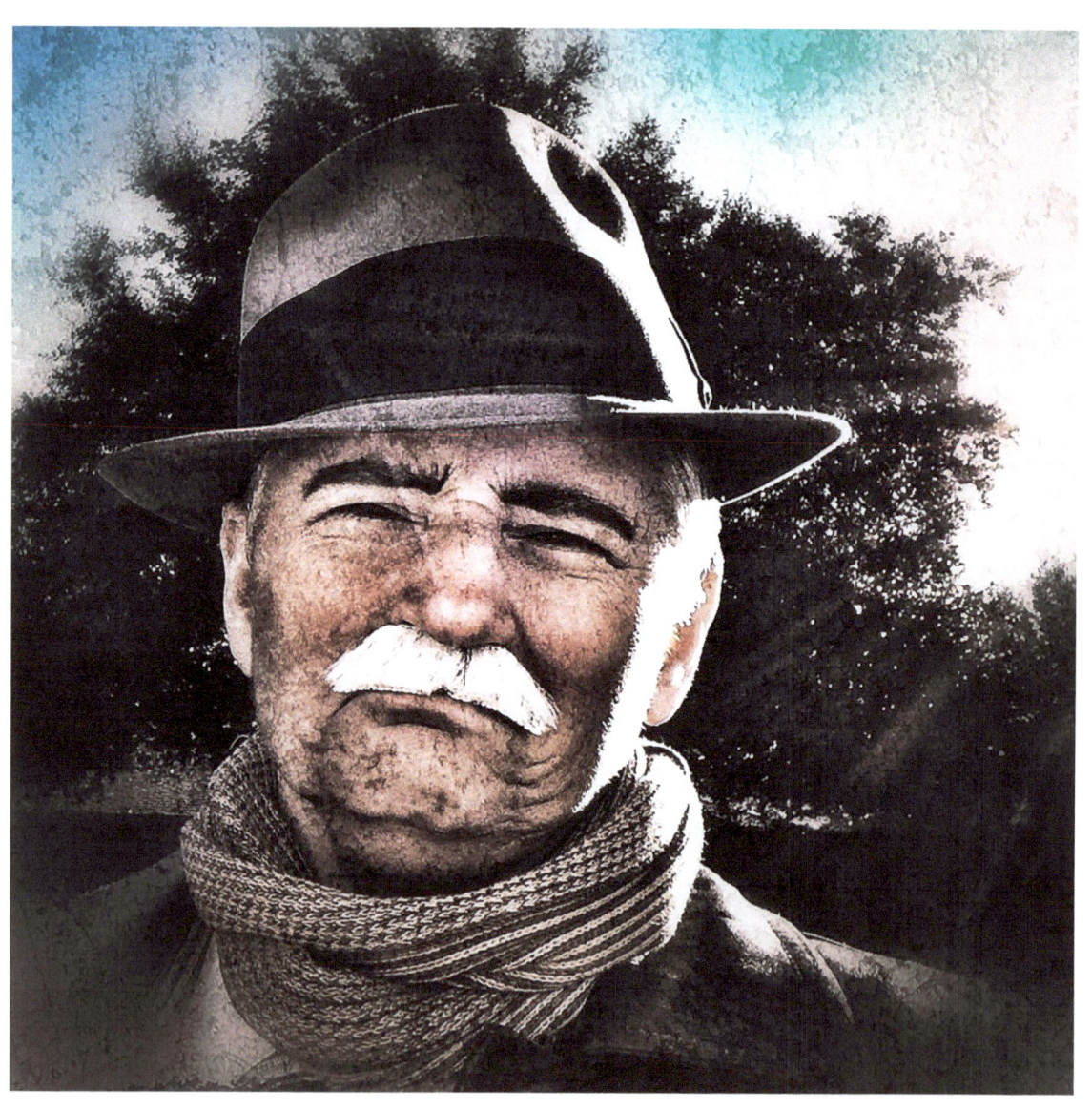

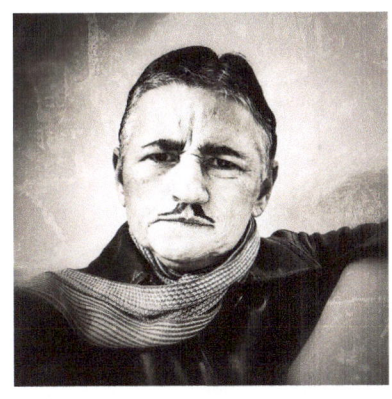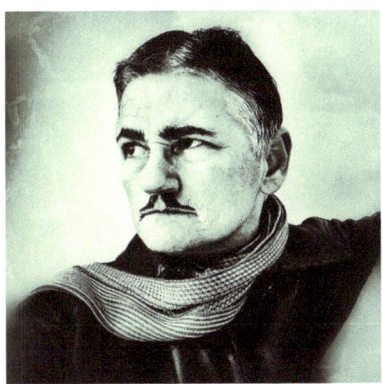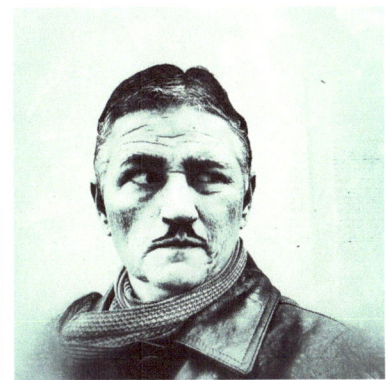

I loved how the vintage photos came out; they were by far my favorites. It was tempting to buy or rent costumes, but finding things in my house to make them look like period costumes was half the fun. Of course, the layers of filters helped.

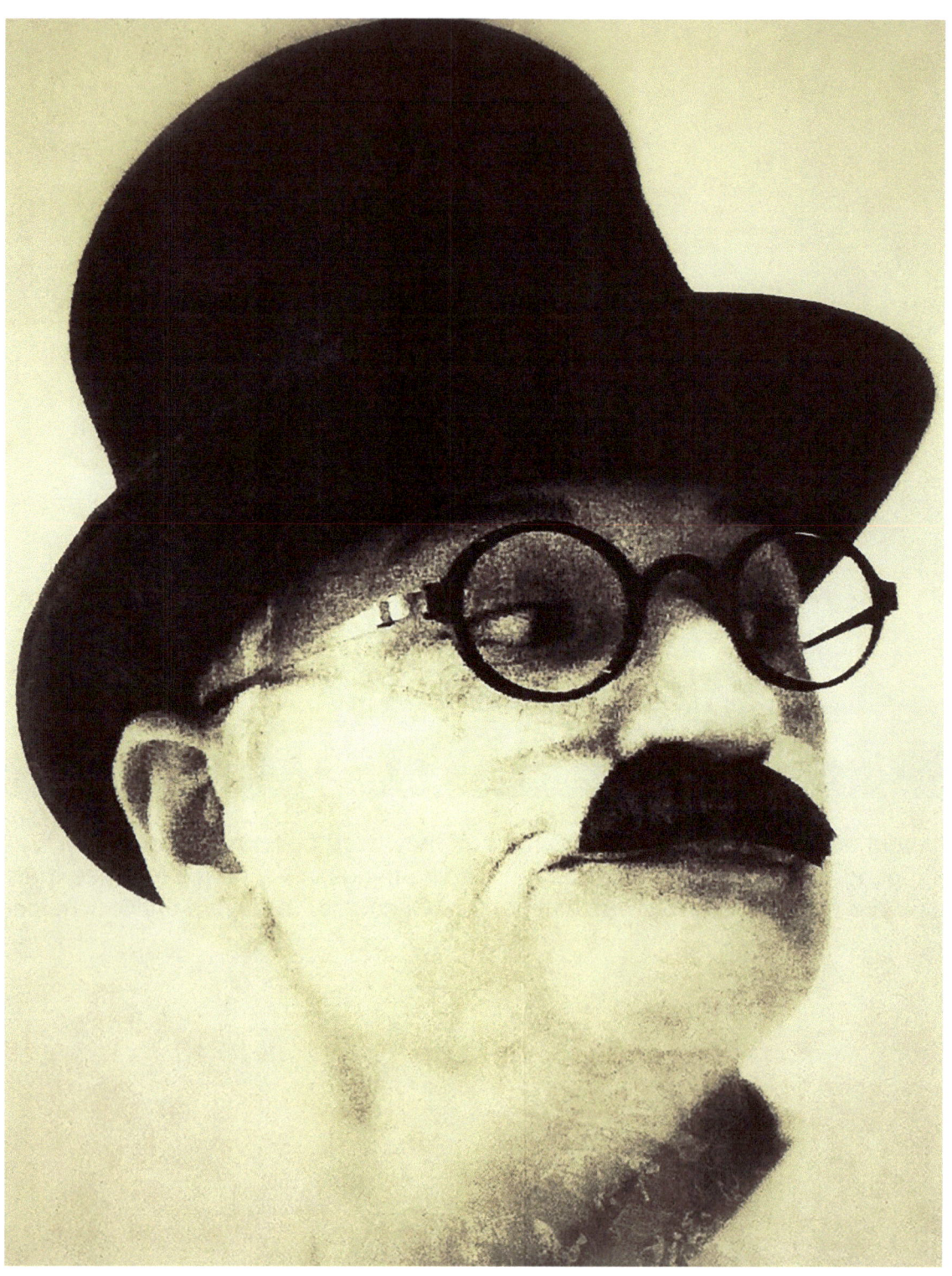

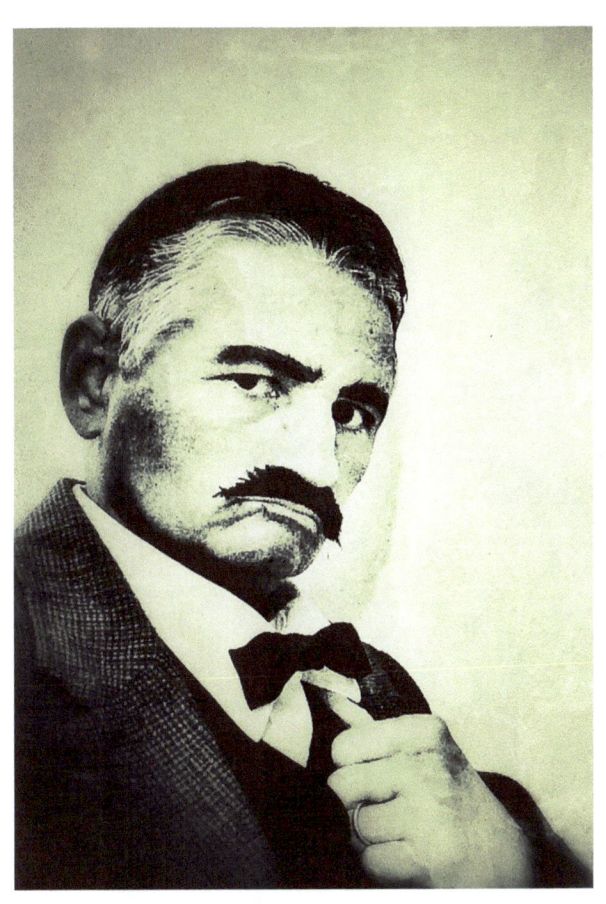
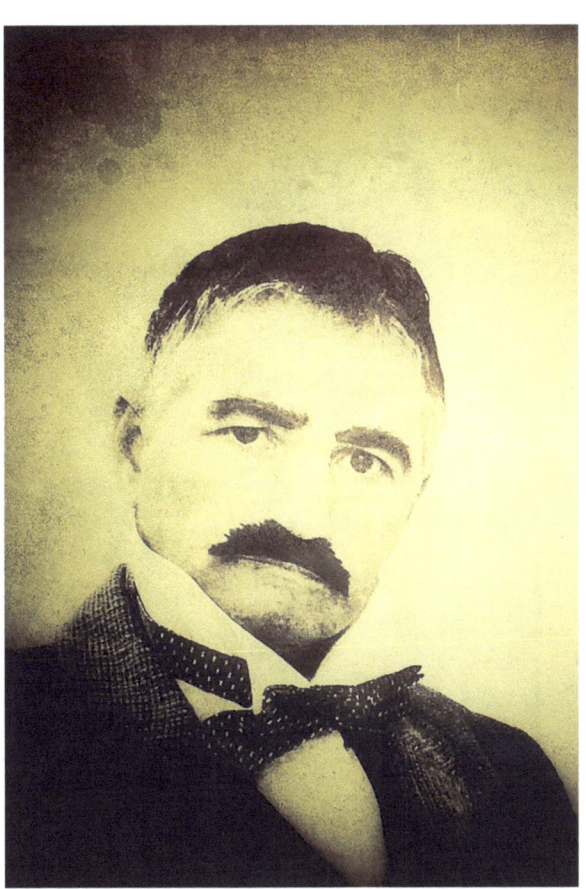

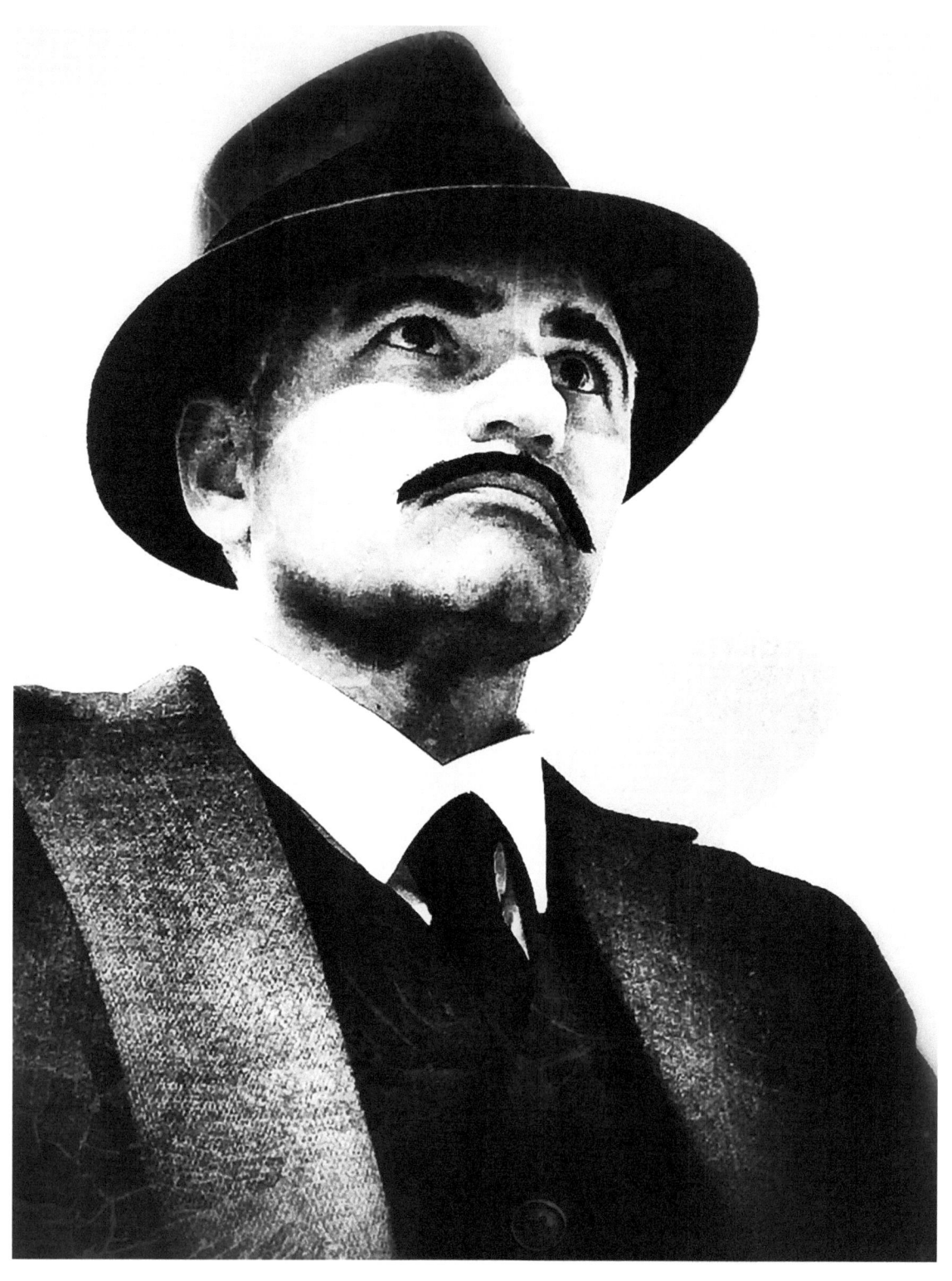

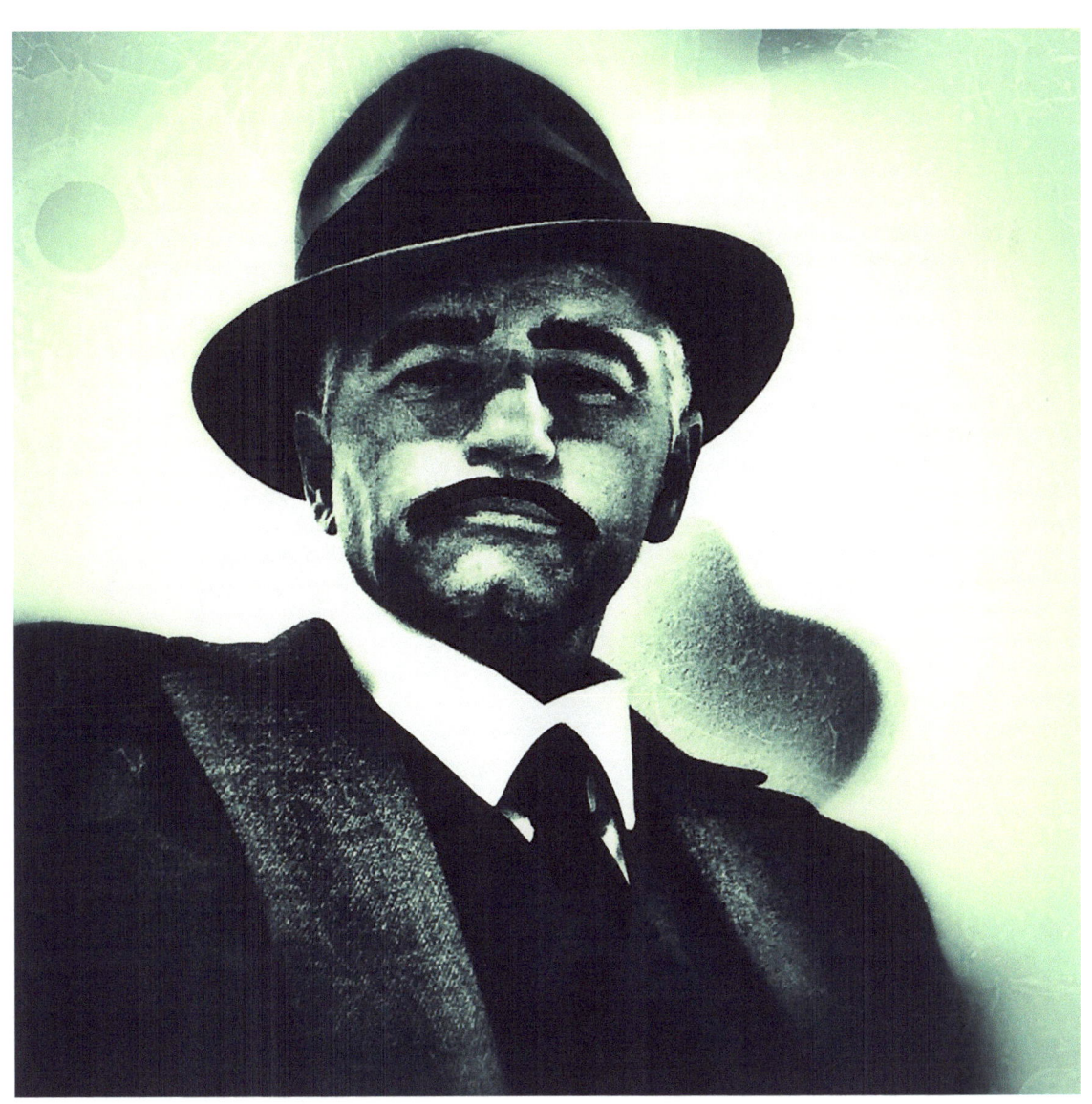

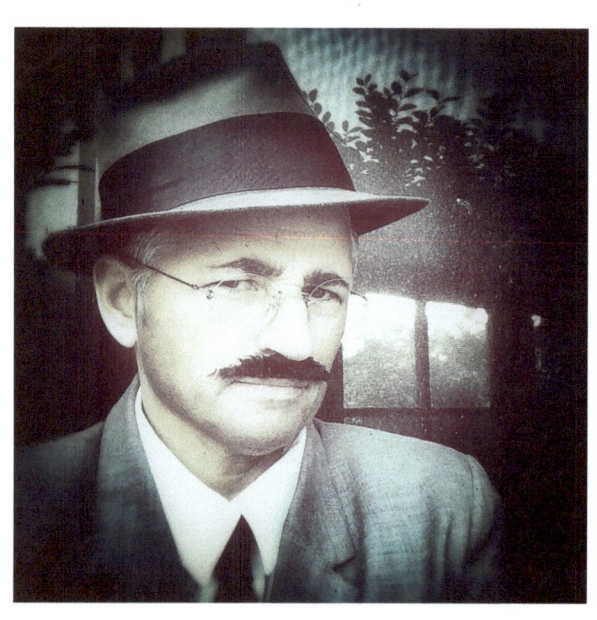 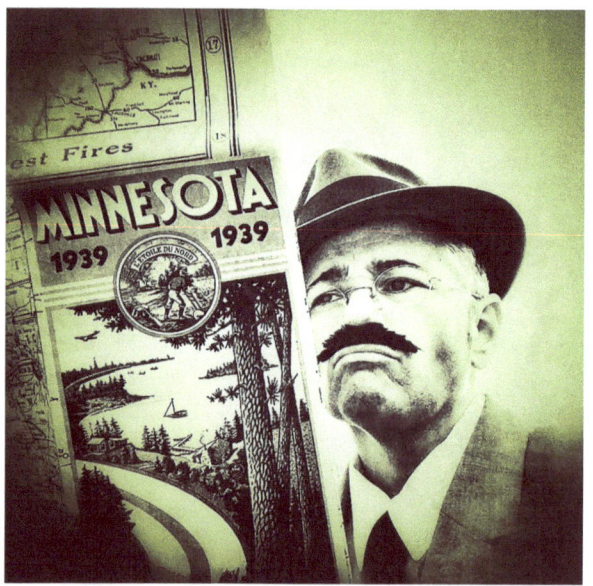

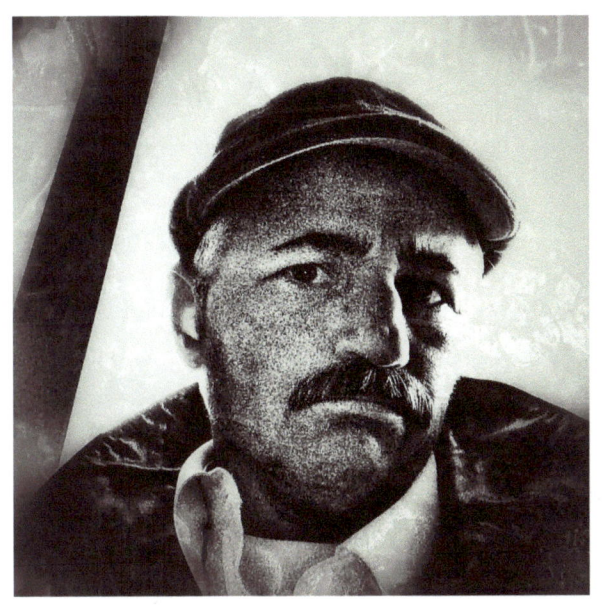
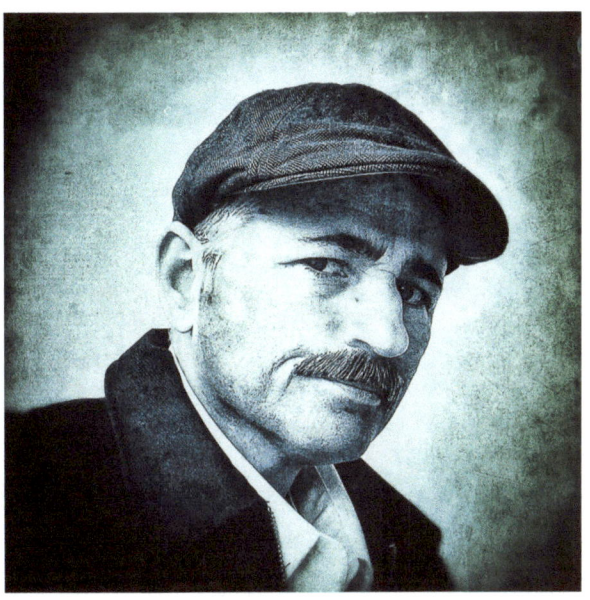
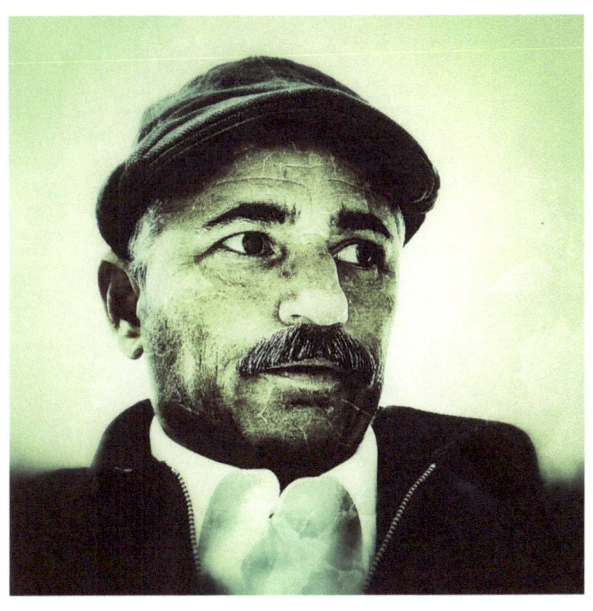
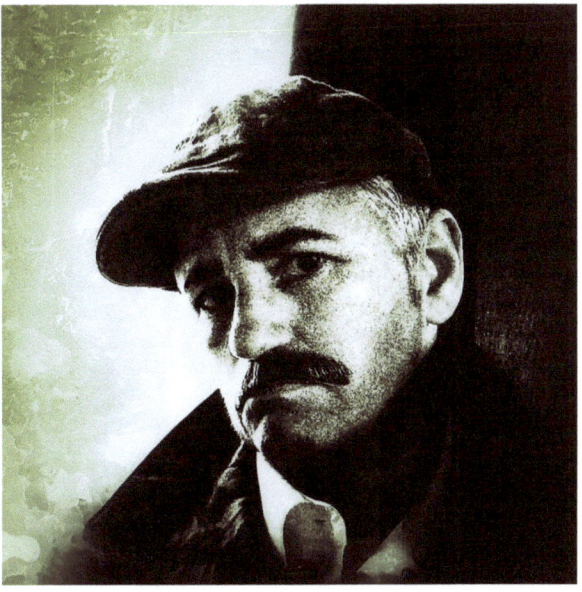

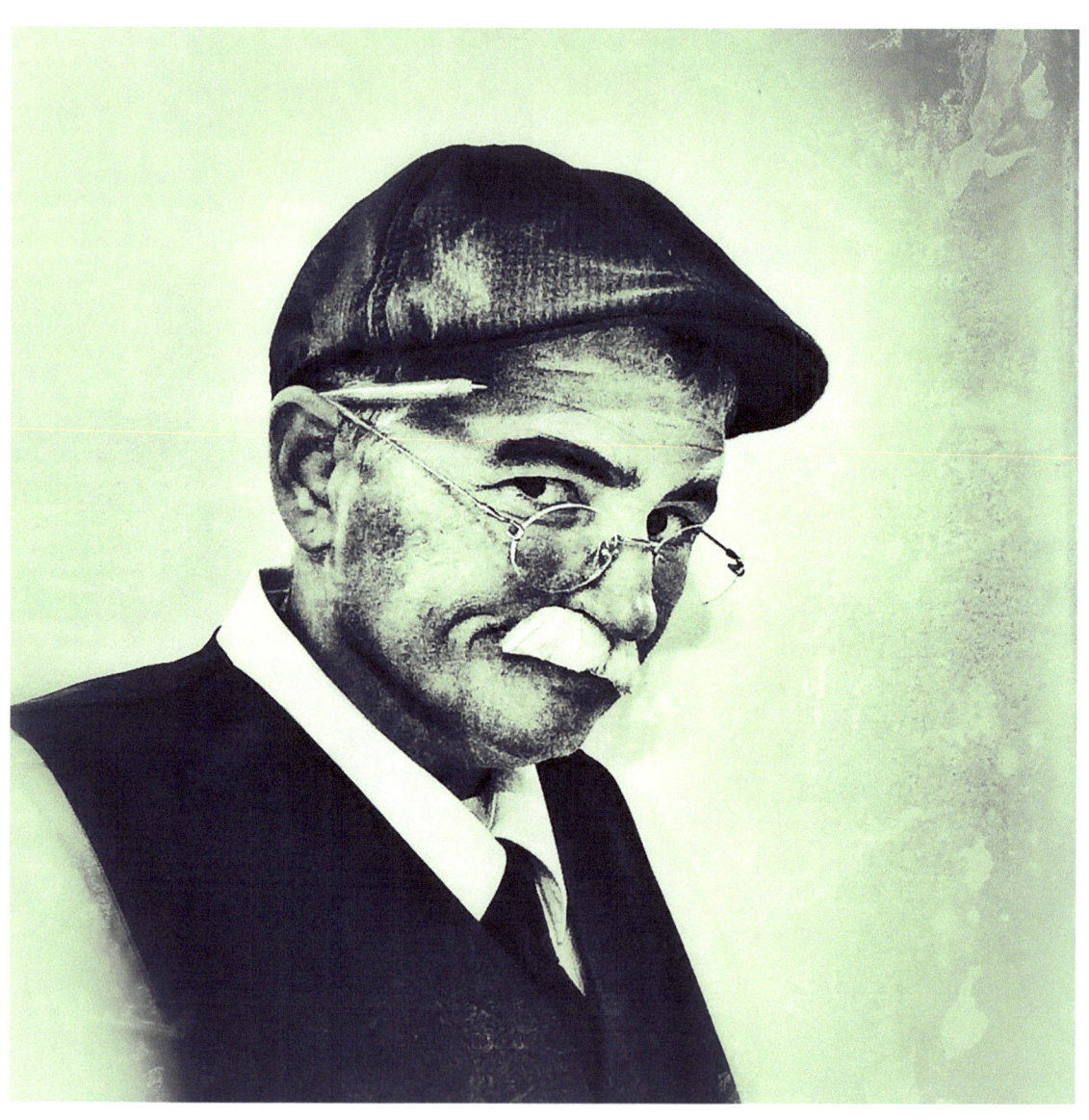

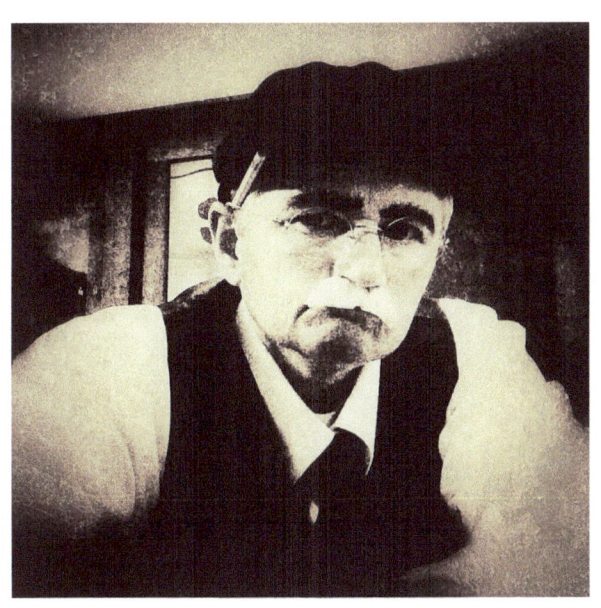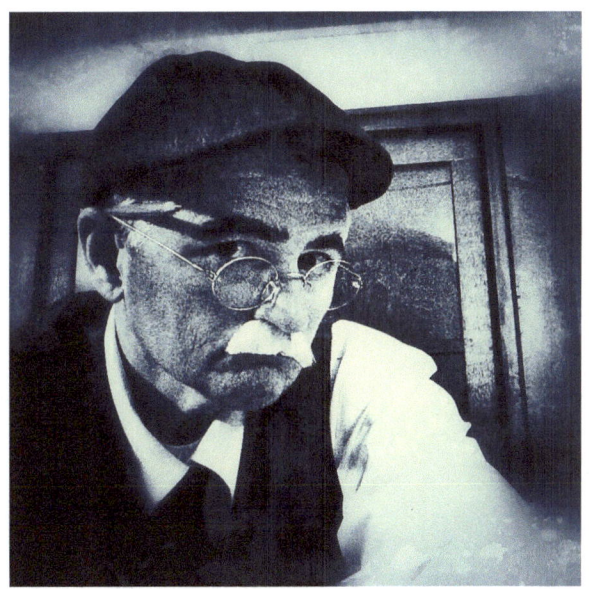

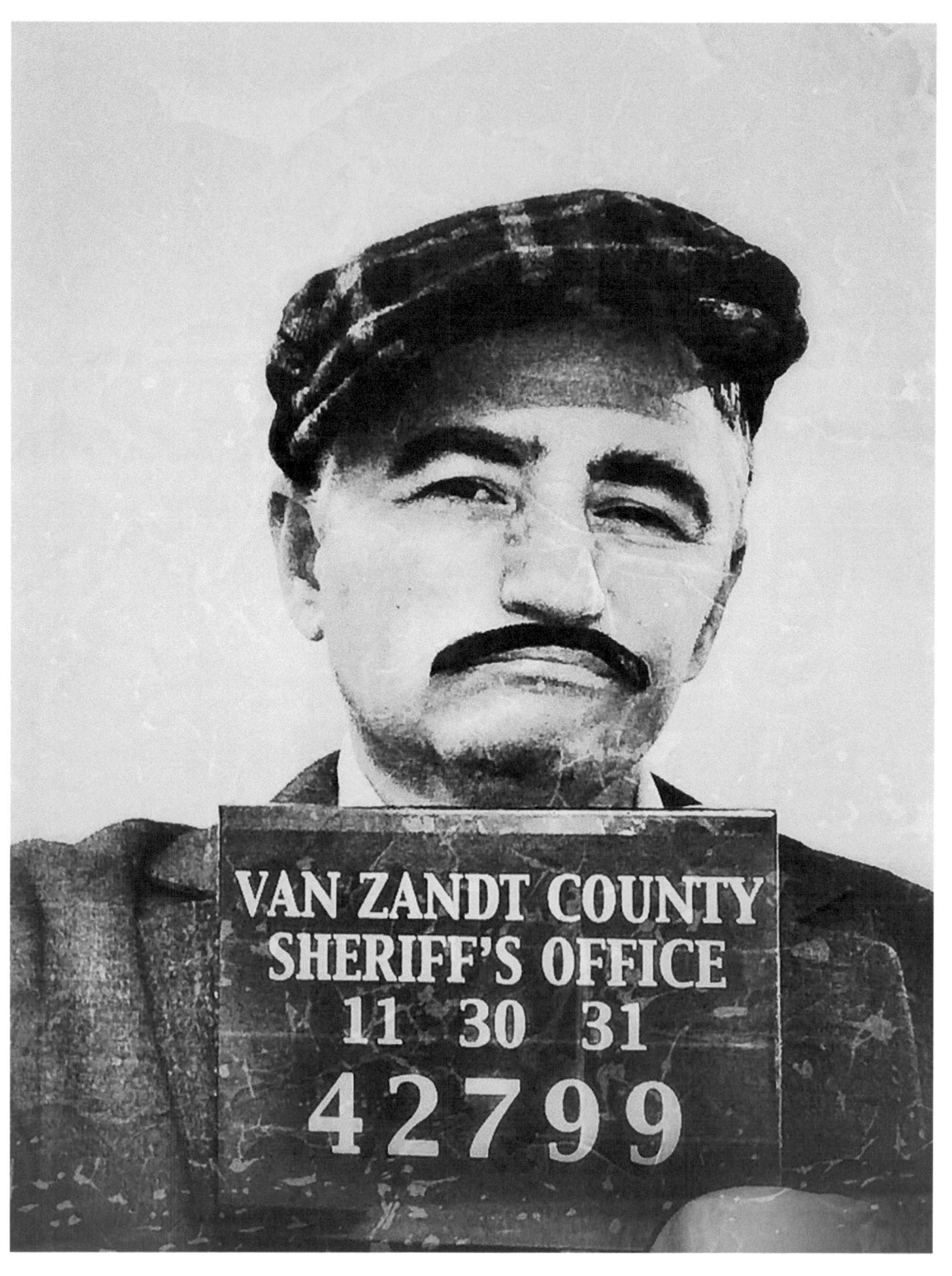

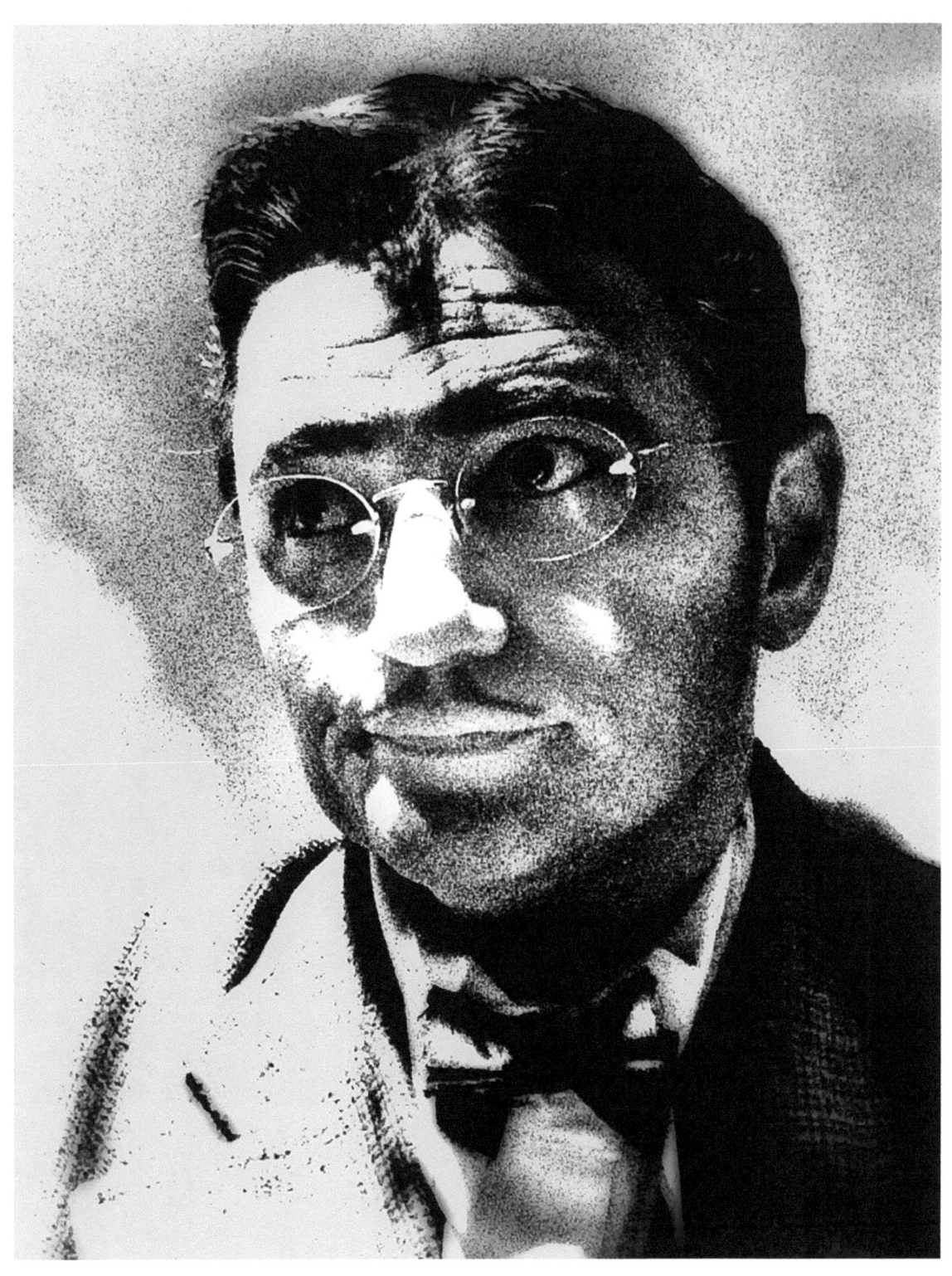

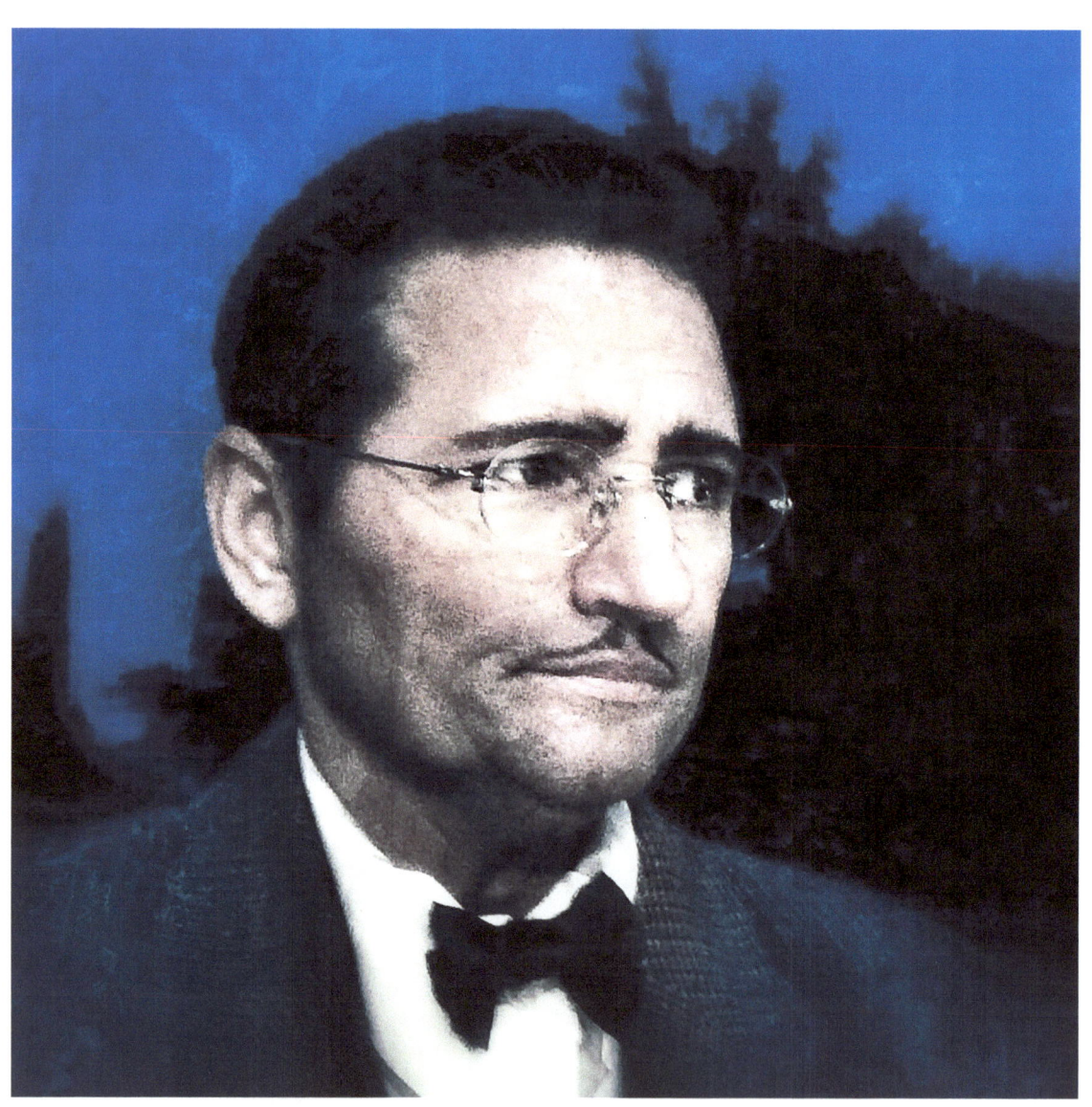

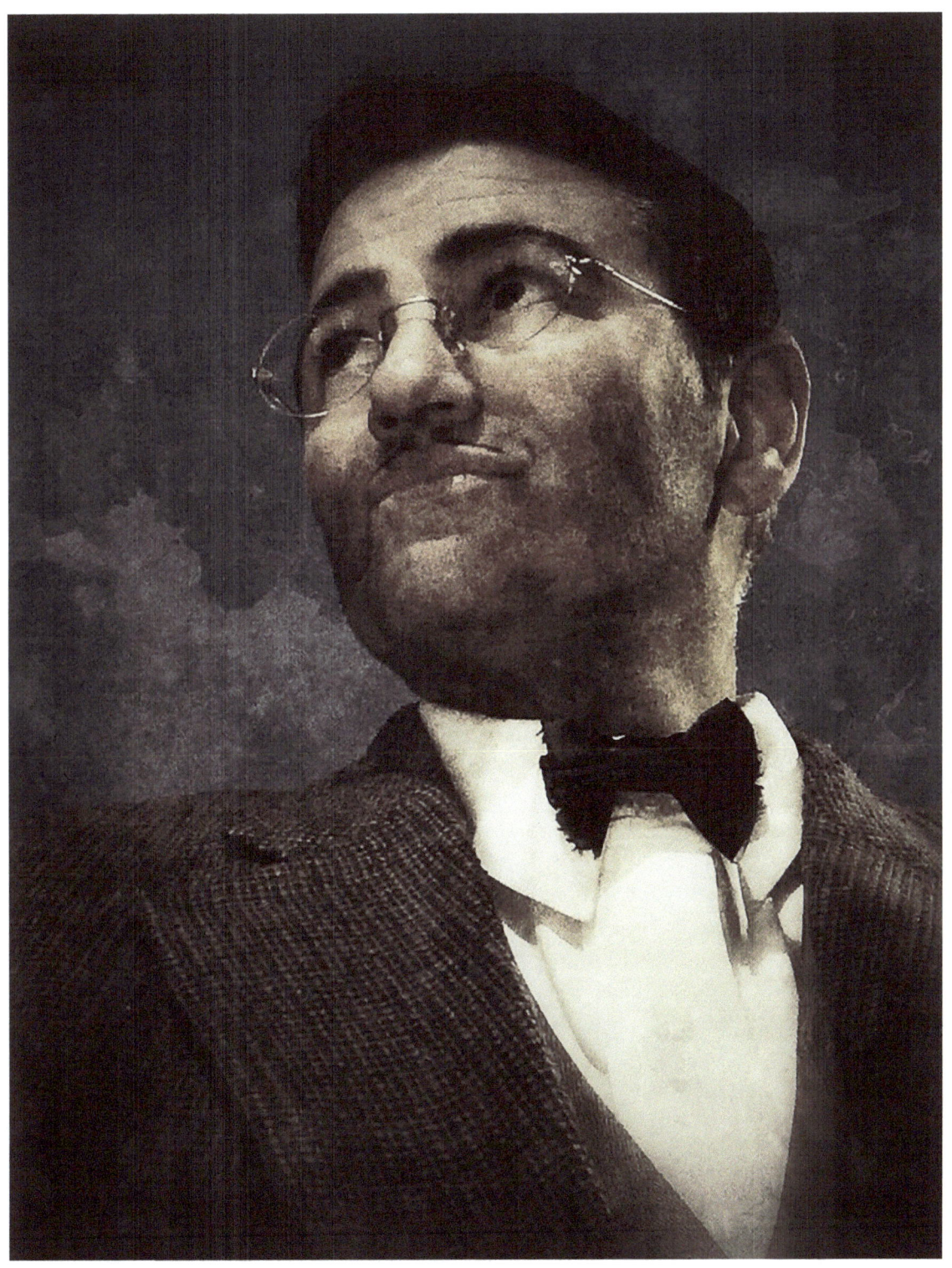

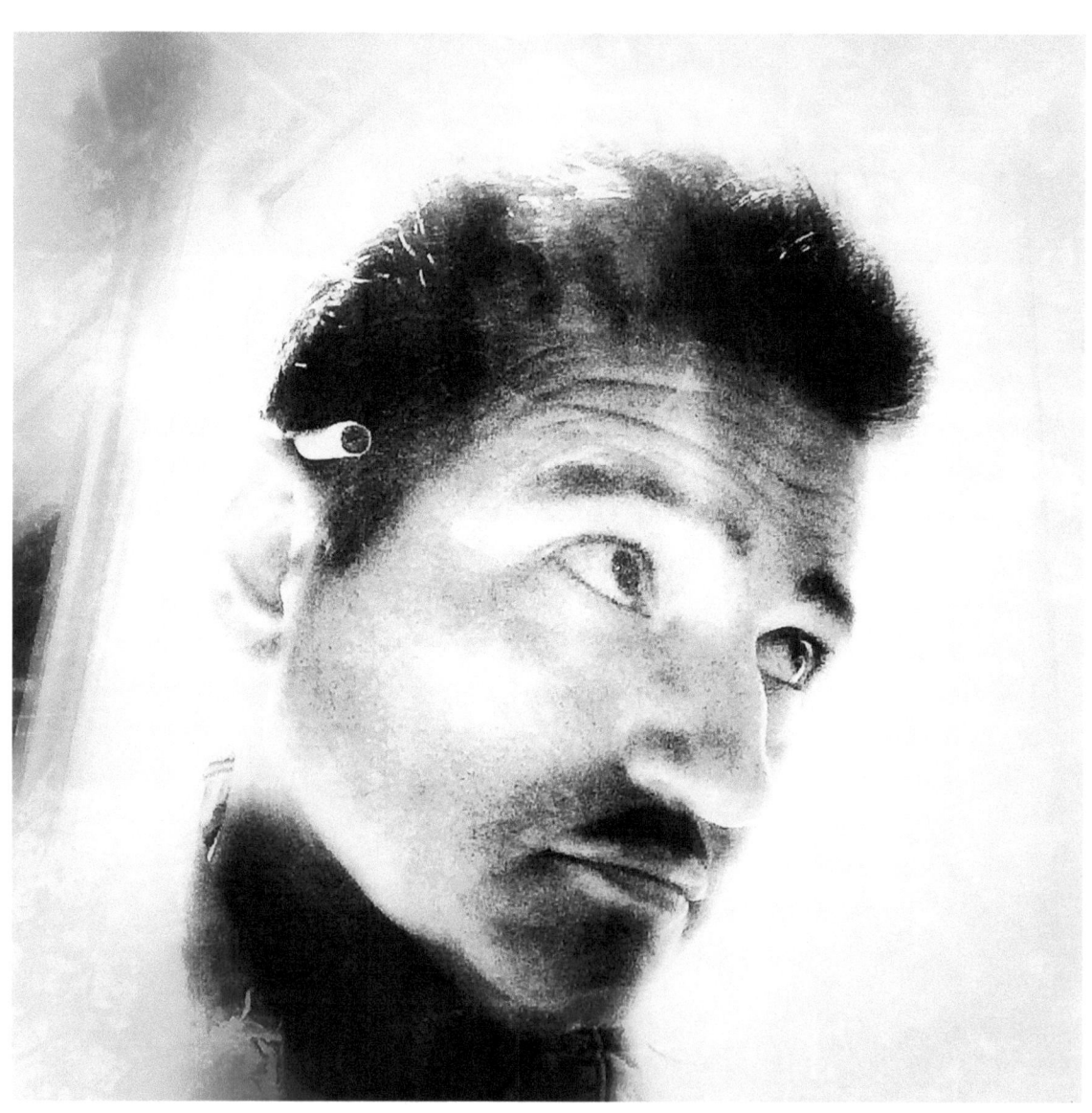

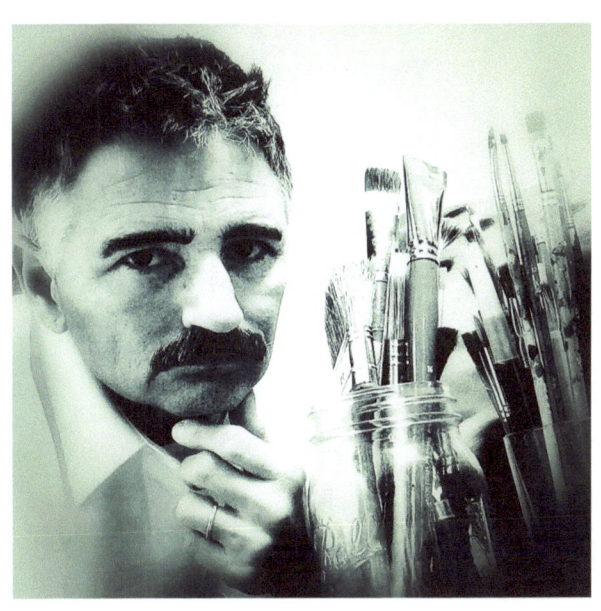

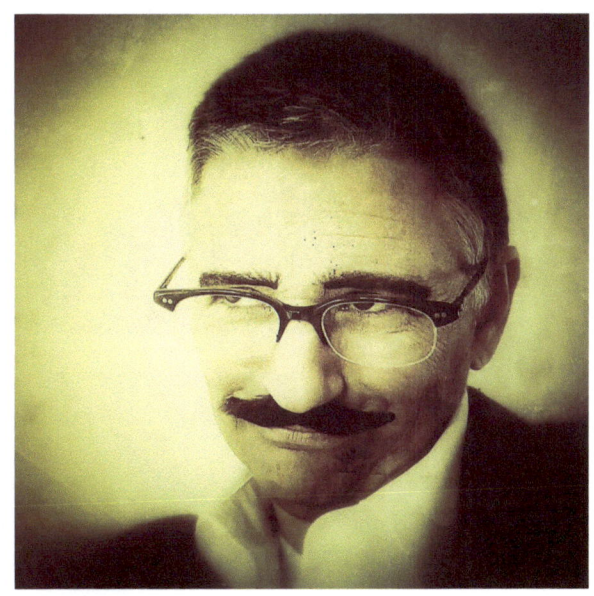

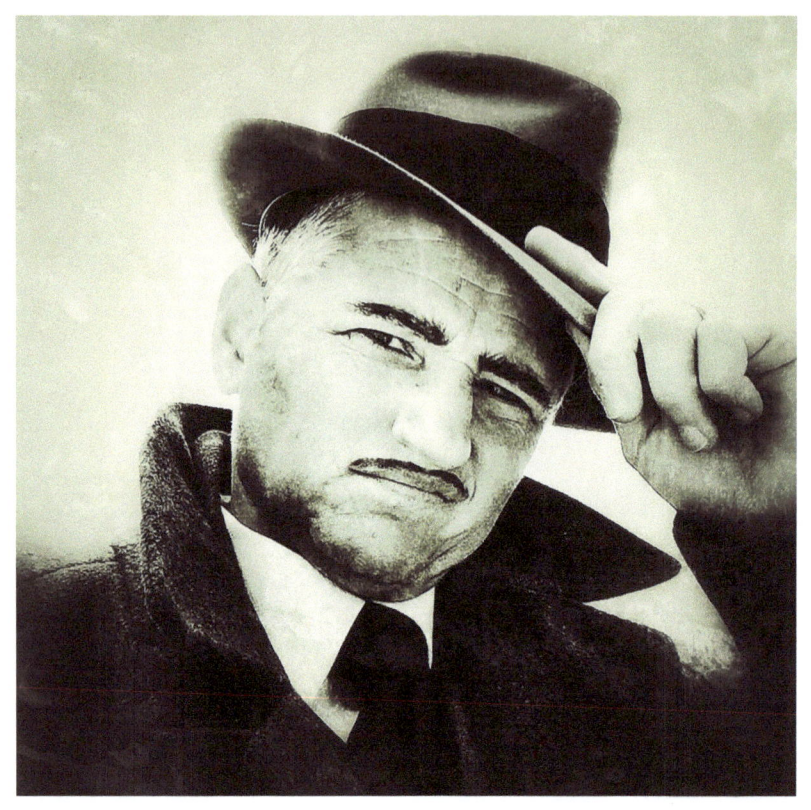

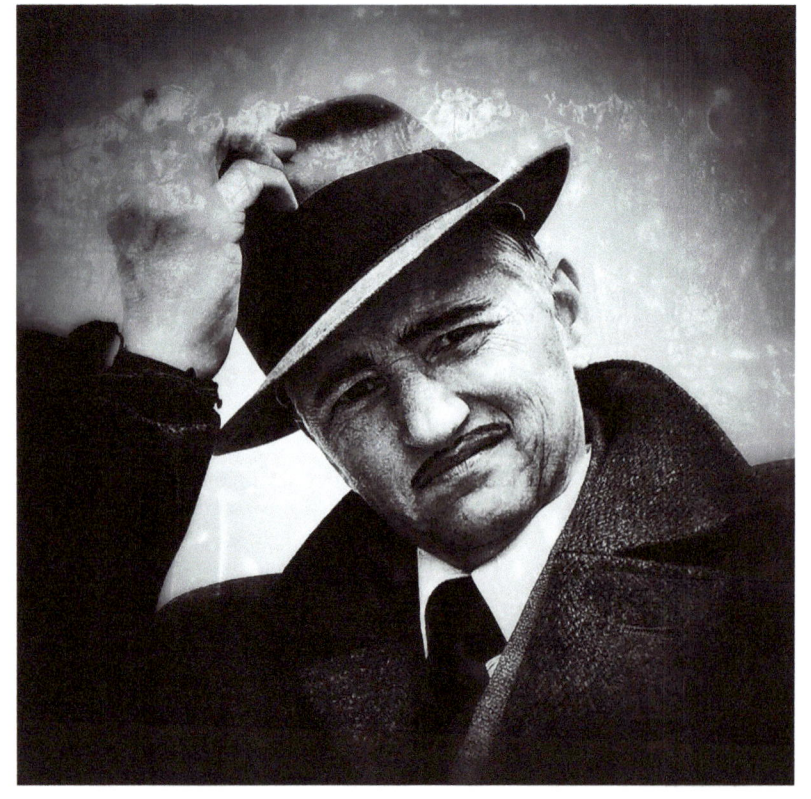

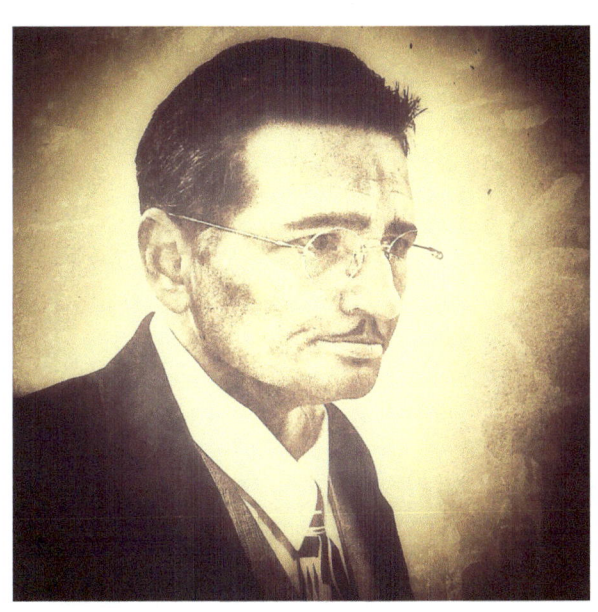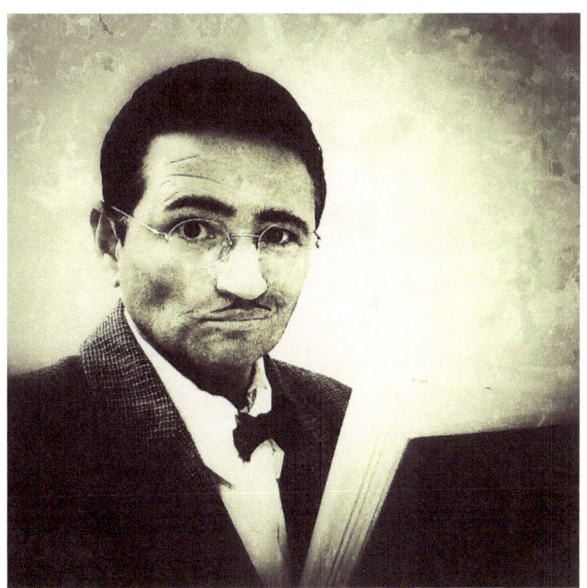

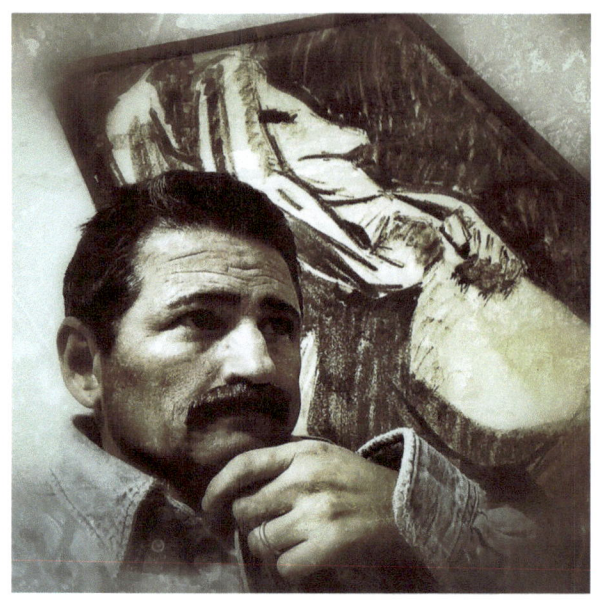
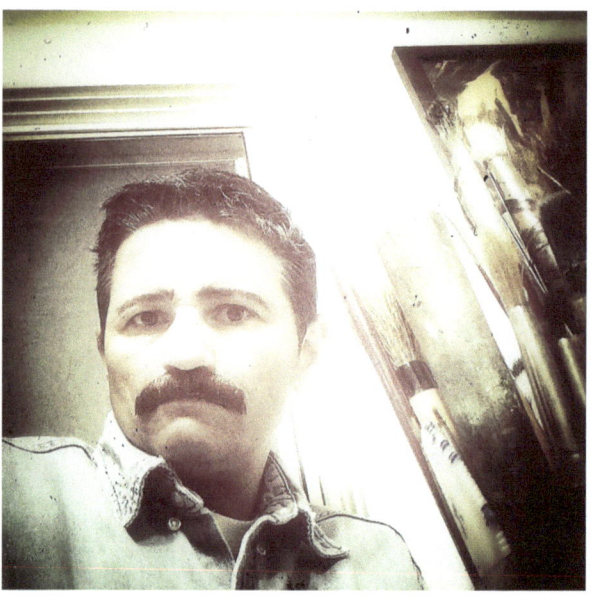
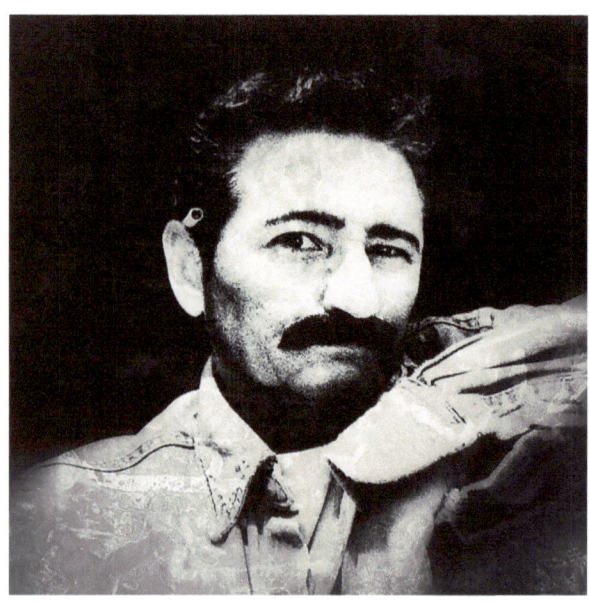
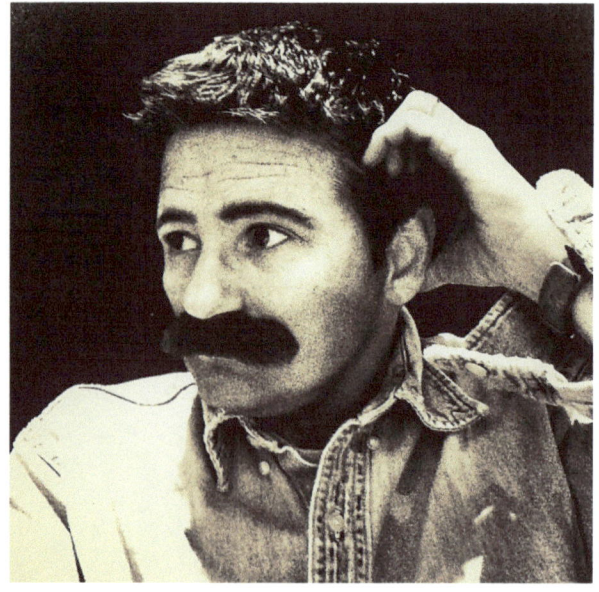

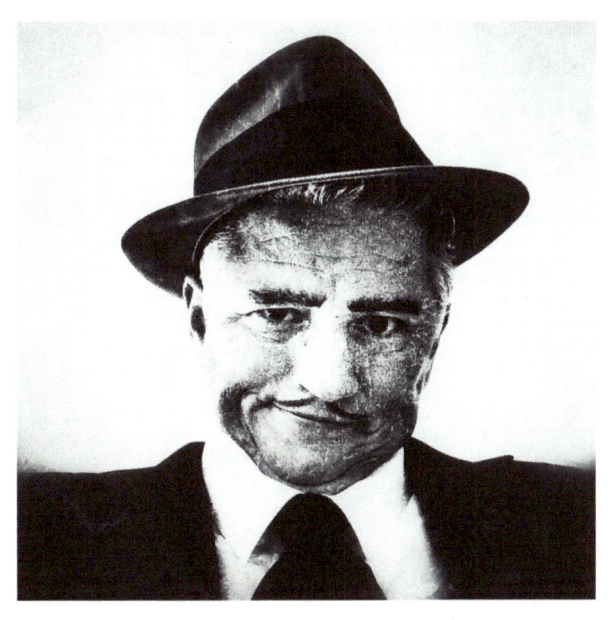

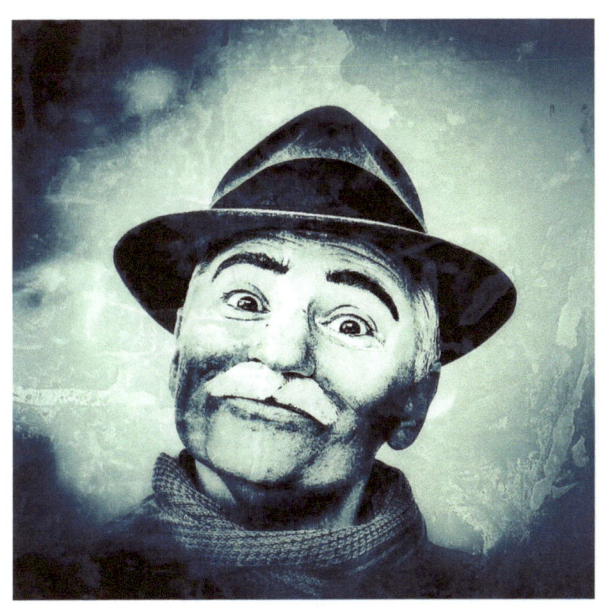

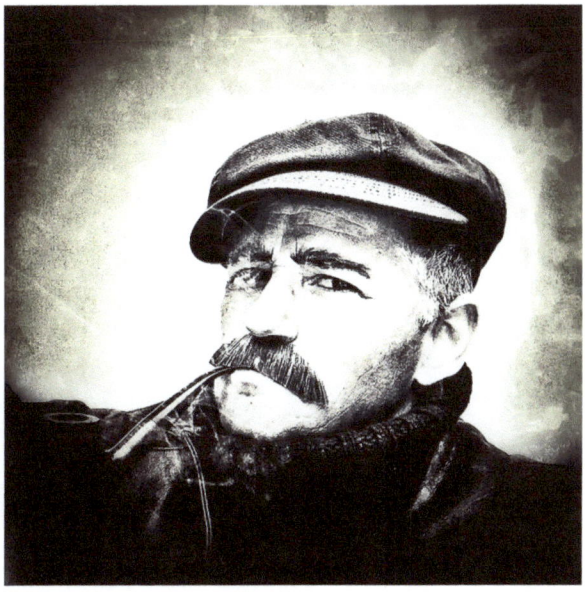

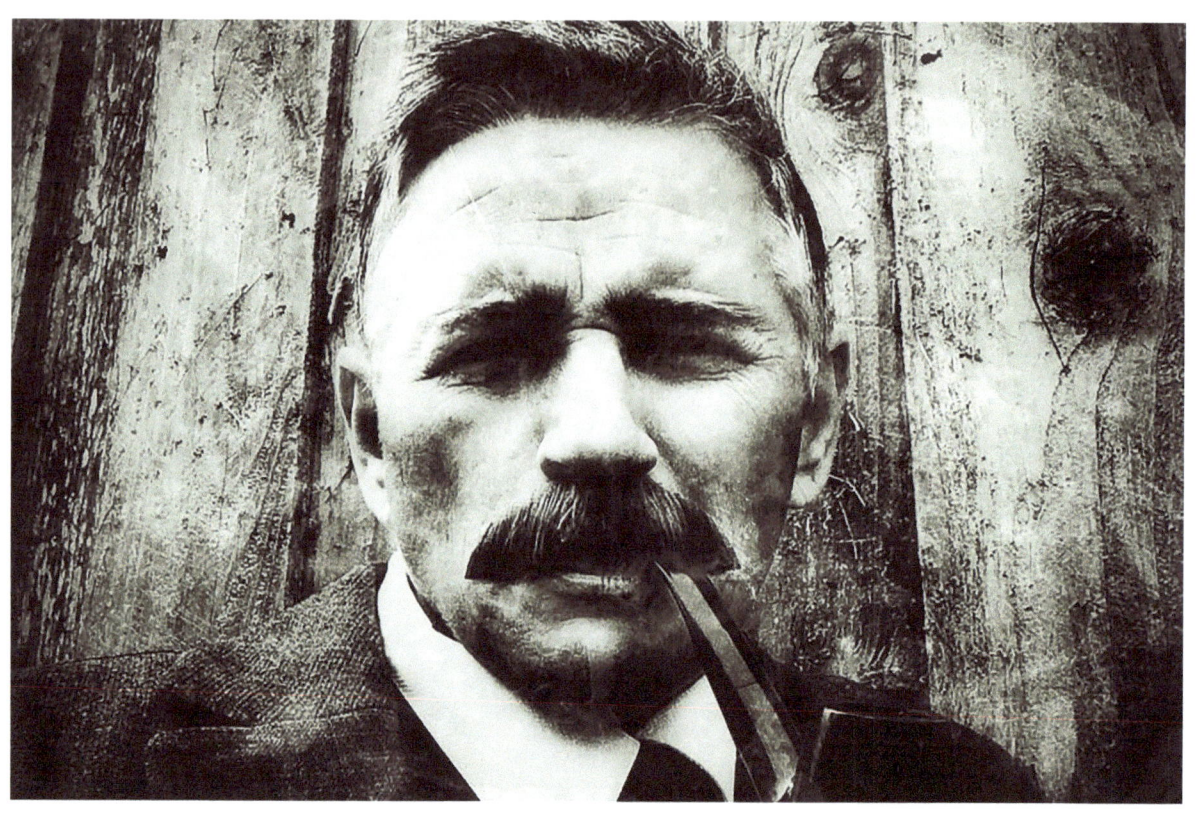

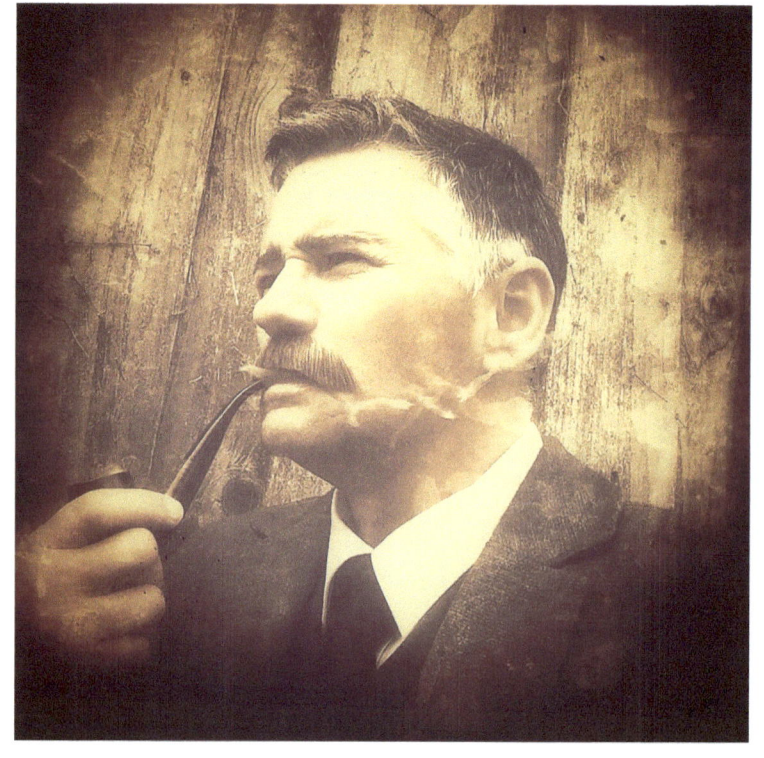

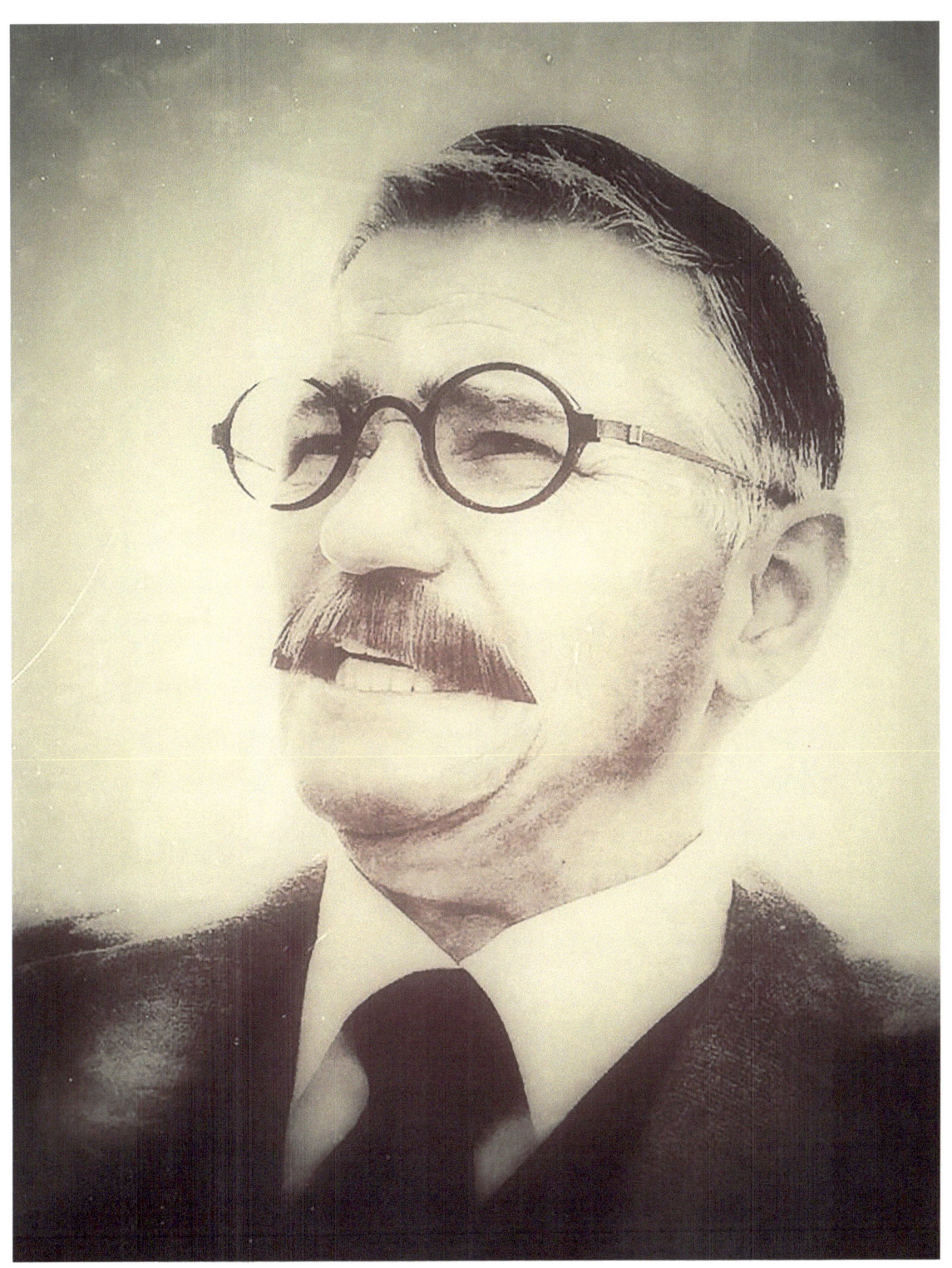

www.ingramcontent.com/pod-product-compliance
Lightning Source LLC
Chambersburg PA
CBHW050742180526
45159CB00003B/1325